KV-687-415

ACKNOWLEDGEMENTS

Thanks to Salford City Housing Department and Councillor David Lancaster for co-operating with the case-study research; to all those in Manchester and Salford who helped with the project and especially Ena Shepherd and Evan Mackenzie.

Thanks to the following people for helping to conduct interviews on the Trinity estate: Tom Casey, Anne Hemmings, Tim Jenkins, Chris Jones, Rachel Mendem, Lisa Ralston, Sue Rigg, Ann-Marie Swain, Tracey Webb, Lara Yude.

Thanks to Dianne Phillips at Manchester Polytechnic for computing the survey data.

Special thanks to Charles McCartan for helping to co-ordinate the case-study project, analyse the results and work on the report.

Shelter thanks the Equal Opportunities Commission for its grant towards the cost of the project.

The project was managed by Shelter's Research Section.

Shelter would also like to thank the advisory committee for the project for giving so generously of their time. The committee was made up of the following members:

Marion Brion, *writer and lecturer at Tottenham College.*
Colette Fagan, *Research Officer, Equal Opportunities Commission.*
Cath Johnson, *Research Officer, Shelter.*
Sheila McKechnie, *Director, Shelter.*
Jenny Morris, *freelance writer and researcher and specialist advisor for the project.*
Matthew Shaps, *Head of Research, Shelter.*
Helene Vancliffe, *Advice Worker at Shelter Housing Aid Centre, Milton Keynes.*
Lindsay Ward, *Campaign Worker at Shelter Leeds.*
Karen Welsh, *Assistant Director of the Rainer Foundation.*

The views expressed in the report are not necessarily those of the EOC ■

LIST OF TABLES

CONTENTS

Chapter one
Less money, less choice   18

■■■ more jobs, still less pay ■■■ black and ethnic minority women in work ■■■ older women and inequality ■■■ women and social policy ■■■ lack of child-care facilities ■■■ women and 'community care' ■■■ social security: who benefits? ■■■ age-related changes in social security ■■■ single payments out – social fund in ■■■ cuts in income for disabled and older women ■■■ changes in board and lodging payments ■■■ changes in taxation ■■■ the poll tax ■■■ conclusion■

Chapter two
Housing options for women   27

■■■ women as home-owners ■■■ women as council tenants ■■■ women as private tenants ■■■ women and housing associations ■■■ young women: leaving home, living where? ■■■ single women: numbers up, needs ignored ■■■ relationship breakdown: where do women go? ■■■ single parents: the forgotten families ■■■ older women: who cares? ■■■ disabled women: homes fit to live in? ■■■ lesbians: no provision ■■■ women in rural areas ■■■ conclusion   ■

Chapter eight
The wider context   **84**

Policy recommendations for Salford City Council   **95**

Conclusion   **97**

Appendix   **98**

Bibliography   **99**

FOREWORD

It is ironic that whilst the view that a woman's place is in the home is still held in some quarters, housing policy remains stubbornly male centred. Women's needs are too often assumed to be the same as family housing needs. When they are considered, it is in the ghetto of special needs. An assumption exists that if they are not in a 'normal' family, women are somehow a problem.

This report has a single message – that women are not the problem – our housing system is. Shelter believes that all women have the right to decent, affordable housing. Yet unfortunately today, many women are forced to remain in unsuitable, poor housing because of a lack of options. Additional problems are raised for particular groups of women, such as black and ethnic minority women, disabled women, lesbians and older women.

Current housing policies, promoting housing for those who can afford to pay rather than those in need, are making it harder for all women to obtain adequate, secure accommodation.

Housing issues for women are part of a wider system of discrimination. Issues such as access to employment and welfare benefits, the lack of childcare facilities, housing design and women's safety both in their own homes and on the streets are all issues which are inextricably linked to women's housing needs and should be raised by policy makers, researchers and campaigning organisations.

It is time that something was done to make sure that all women have access to decent, affordable housing. Shelter has a special responsibility to pursue the issues raised in this report. So do all housing providers and policy makers in Britain today. The time has come to get on with it ∎

Sheila McKechnie.
Director, Shelter.

8

SUMMARY OF THE REPORT

This report looks at women's access to housing in Britain today and the effects of current policies on women's ability to get access to suitable housing, using both existing research and original research material carried out specifically for this report.

The report highlights the issue of inequality in access to housing between women and men, opening the way for further discussions about these inequalities and action for change among housing providers, policy makers and all those concerned with women's housing experiences.

The report points out that housing policy today continues to be based on the assumption that the nuclear family (that is, a man, a woman and dependent children) is the 'normal' living unit, despite the fact that only 28% of households today conform to this pattern. This assumption has a detrimental effect on women who live without men, and also women within 'conventional families' whose needs are not automatically met within these units.

The report also highlights the fact that current housing policies, which promote home-ownership at the expense of public housing, are reducing women's range of housing options even further.

The report makes recommendations to central government, the Equal Opportunities Commission, local authorities and other housing providers, calling for policy changes to bring about equality for women in access to housing.

Part I of the report gives an overview of women's access to housing in Britain today, using existing research and statistics. It makes important links between women's access to income and employment and their access to housing, showing that women are disadvantaged in the housing market because of their low incomes and poor employment prospects.

Part I is illustrated with a number of case studies obtained from housing advice centres and other voluntary agencies. In order to protect the anonymity of the individuals referred to, names and any identifiable factors have been changed.

Part II presents the findings from a small-scale case study research project conducted in Salford during 1989 and early 1990. The case study focuses on

9

women's access to housing on the Trinity estate in Salford and on the effects of one aspect of national housing policy – privatisation. The research project is the first of its kind to examine the effects of privatisation on women's access to housing.

The report ends with a series of policy recommendations for Salford City Council, drawn up in the light of the case study findings, and a general conclusion to the research ■

POLICY RECOMMENDATIONS

The policy recommendations detailed below do not represent a blueprint for an ideal housing policy. Rather, they are general recommendations which are designed to raise awareness about the discrimination women face in access to housing among policy makers, housing providers and the public at large.

Central Government – Housing Policy Recommendations

1. The Government should ensure that all housing providers are complying with the provisions of Section 29 of the 1975 Sex Discrimination Act. This provision says it is unlawful to discriminate by sex in the provision of facilities and services, including accommodation. This should involve ensuring that equal opportunities statements are issued which private land-lords, housing associations and local authorities would be advised to comply with. These statements should also cover money lenders in the home-buying market, such as building societies and banks, ensuring that the policy is applied consistently to all consumers.

2. The Government should urgently halt and reverse their policy of encouraging the privatisation of council housing.

3. Sufficient financial resources must be provided by central government to enable local authorities to provide decent and affordable housing for all those in need. This will involve changing the present structure of housing finance and increasing investment in public housing.

4. The Government should consider urgently amending the 1985 Housing Act, Part III, extending the 'official' definitions of homelessness and 'priority need'. In particular, the Government should ensure that single people, young people, women escaping violence and people experiencing harass-

11

ment and abuse on the grounds of race, sex and sexuality are covered by the homelessness legislation. The legislation should also include all those whose capital and income are below the level required to obtain adequate and suitable housing in the private housing market.

5. Government statistics on homelessness, housing tenure, housing conditions, household types and related issues should include a breakdown by sex and race wherever possible. They should also include details about age, disability and sexuality wherever possible.

6. Government policy should be geared towards encouraging local authorities and other housing providers to provide varied and improved services in respect of housing to suit the needs of different household types. Local authorities and other housing providers should be encouraged to introduce and improve monitoring procedures by age, disability, race, sex and sexuality wherever possible.

Local authorities and other housing providers should also be encouraged to improve allocation procedures, transfers, waiting list procedures and homelessness procedures with regard to equality of opportunity for all. This would enable policy makers and housing providers to ensure that local and national housing needs are being met.

7. The Government should introduce legislation to require local authorities to produce a strategy for providing housing for those people covered by the community care legislation.

Central Government – Social Security Policy Recommendations

1. Social security benefits, including Income Support, Housing Benefit and Community Charge Rebate, should be responsive to the needs of women. The Department of Social Security (DSS) should monitor and keep under review the need for entitlement based on the woman's sole income and issues such as benefit levels, costs of childcare and entitlement on relationship breakdown.

2. Benefits should be designed to secure and maintain women's access to housing. In particular, the DSS should review the effects of the social fund and maximum eligibility for housing benefit and community charge rebate.

3. Housing benefit should be increased to meet market rents.

4. Women in refuges should be eligible to receive a boarder's premium. Any shortfalls in refuges' income should be met by the DSS.

5. The carer's premium to be introduced in October 1990 should be increased from £10 per week to a realistic level.

Equal Opportunities Commission (EOC)

1. The EOC, in conjunction with other relevant bodies, should use their powers to draw up guidelines for good practice for local authorities, other housing providers and mortgage lenders to remove discrimination and ensure women's equality in access to housing.

2. The EOC should use their investigative powers under Section 57 of the 1975 Sex Discrimination Act to explore potential discrimination in housing provision.

Public Housing Providers

Recommendations for local authorities and housing associations

1. Public housing providers should pay heed to their statutory duties regarding the elimination of sexual discrimination under sections 29-31 of the Sex Discrimination Act.

2. Public housing providers should have a comprehensive equal opportunities policy covering housing provision and related services. These policies should be drawn up in conjunction with targeted groups and backed up by positive measures to improve services in respect of equal opportunities. This would include staff training and regular liaison with targeted groups.

3. Public housing providers should issue 'good practice guidelines' for all housing officers, paying particular attention to equality of opportunity and eliminating discrimination on the grounds of age, disability, race, sex and sexuality.

4. Housing programmes and policies should be geared towards meeting local housing needs. This will involve all public housing providers looking urgently at existing policies on allocations procedures, homelessness, transfers and waiting lists with a view to improving these procedures in respect of equal opportunities policies and statements.

5. Public housing providers should introduce monitoring or improve existing

monitoring by age, disability, race, sex and sexuality wherever possible for all housing services including homelessness applications, waiting lists, transfers and allocations. Where monitoring procedures already exist, housing providers should endeavour to improve and extend these procedures.

6. Public housing providers should develop and effect policies and procedures for complaints about harassment and discrimination on grounds of age, disability, race, sex and sexuality in the provision of services.

7. All aspects of public housing provision and management should take into account the needs of disabled people. New build and improvement programmes should be designed with the needs of disabled people in mind.

8. Public housing providers should employ flexible policies allowing succession to a tenancy. Succession rights should not be limited to marital or close family ties but should include people who lived with the previous tenant for a specified period, for example, six months. This would enable single women and lesbian partners to succeed to a tenancy.

Recommendations specifically for local authorities

1. Local authorities must urgently halt and reverse trends in selling off council stock to private developers.

2. Local authorities should halt and reverse policies of closing down specialist women's units. All local authorities should employ women's officers and/or establish a women's unit. The officers/women's unit should liaise with targeted groups in the community and feed back information on the housing needs and experiences of these groups.

3. The needs of women and particular groups of women such as black and ethnic minority women, disabled women, lesbians, older women and single women must be integrated within general allocations policies, in conjunction with representatives of targeted groups.

4. Local authorities' points systems should be amended to include priority for single women in housing need. This could include awarding additional points for shared rooms, lack of amenities and disrepair.

5. Local authorities should set up Adaptations and Disability Units within housing departments, bringing together relevant staff to serve disabled tenants and owners. Accurate and quickly accessible data should be available to determine which properties are accessible to disabled people.

Mortgage lenders

1. Banks, building societies and other mortgage lenders should apply consistent policies to all borrowers, bearing in mind the provisions of Section 29 of the 1975 Sex Discrimination Act.

2. Lenders should not apply for repossession orders against women remaining in the home where arrears have been accumulated by their male partners ■

PART I

Women's access to housing: an overview

chapter one

LESS MONEY, LESS CHOICE

Existing research confirms the importance of the relationship between income and access to housing. The English House Condition Survey (1986), for example, showed that a total of 2,868,000 houses in England – 15% of the housing stock – were in poor condition. The survey confirmed that *'poor housing is related above all, to low income'*.

In general, women are poorer than men. Their low incomes and poor employment opportunities affect their ability to live in the kind of housing they want. While chapters two, three and four look in some detail at women's housing experiences, this chapter sets the scene by outlining women's general economic and social position. The chapter focuses particularly on recent legislative changes and ends with a look at how women are losing out because of the introduction of the poll tax.

More jobs – still less pay

Approximately 65% of women (and 88% of men) between the ages of 16 and 64 in Britain today are either in paid work or seeking paid work. Statistics show that the proportion of working women is becoming increasingly similar to the proportion of working men. Women now make up 40% of the labour force, and their share is expected to have increased to 44% by the end of the century (*Equal Opportunities Commission, 1989*).

The Equal Opportunities Commission (EOC) points out that falling birth rates in the 1970s mean that the number of young people aged between 16 and 25 is expected to fall by 1.4 million between 1987 and the year 2000, creating huge labour shortages. As a result, many firms are currently targeting women as a key group to be encouraged into the labour force in the 1990s.

However, despite the existence of equal pay and sex discrimination legislation in Britain, women continue to be confined to low-paid and low status work in comparison to men. Research by the Low Pay Unit shows that throughout the 1980s women working full-time earned approximately two-thirds of the wages that men earned (*Low Pay Unit, 1988*).

Women's jobs are largely concentrated in traditionally female occupations, such as clerical work, catering, cleaning and shop work. About half of all women work part-time compared to just five per cent of men. In 1986 just 0.3% of companies were chaired by women and only 6.2% of senior managers were women (*Labour Force Survey, 1987*). The EOC say that only limited change is expected in this pattern of occupational distribution by the mid-1990s (*EOC, 1989*).

Black and ethnic minority women in work

There are important differences between women of different ethnic origins in terms of access to employment, unemployment rates and earnings. The Labour Force Surveys between 1985 and 1987 show that two-thirds of West Indian and Indian women work full-time compared with just over half of white women. However, black and ethnic minority people are more likely to be unemployed than white people (*Employment Gazette, 1988*).

Black and ethnic minority women are more likely than white women to be working in the health services and in parts of the manufacturing sector where pay is notoriously low. West Indian women are only half as likely as white women to be in managerial and professional grades and more likely to be in manual work rather than non-manual work (*Employment Gazette, 1988*).

Research on earnings shows that among men there are clear differences in favour of white men at all job levels. Among women there is little difference between earnings on the basis of ethnic origin. However, black and ethnic minority women are in the same position as white women when compared to their male counterparts, with generally lower wages at all levels (see, for example, *Colin Brown, 1982, Karen Clarke, 1988*).

Older women and inequality

The inequalities women face in access to income and employment are carried over into old age. Despite the growth in occupational pensions, about six million older people claim supplementary benefit or housing benefit out of a pensioner population of 9.5 million. Because women are less likely than men to have full-time and secure employment, they are less likely to have occupational pensions and are more likely to be heavily dependent on the state for financial support in terms of state retirement pensions, income support and housing benefit.

Women and social policy

Social policy researchers and writers say that social policies have traditionally been built around assumptions about the 'family' and women's role within the family. In particular, it has always been assumed that the 'nuclear family' – a man, a woman and his dependent children – is the normal living unit and that within 'families', women are first, and foremost, wives and mothers despite the fact that more women are going out to work than ever before. Linked to this is the assumption that women are financially supported by working husbands or partners (see, for example, *Jennifer Dale and Peggy Foster, 1986, Gillian Pascall, 1986*).

Popular perceptions of family life today see the family unit as one in which all members benefit equally in terms of income and other resources. However, as studies have consistently shown, women do not always have an equal access to income and other resources within families, particularly where they are financially dependent on a male partner (see, for example, J*an Pahl, 1982, Hilary Graham, 1986*).

Many women do not fit the assumptions on which social policies have traditionally been based. Today, less than three in ten households conform to the traditional nuclear family. Social and demographic changes in the post-war period, such as greater longevity, later marriages and increasing rates of divorce and separation, have resulted in more women living without a male partner, at least for parts of their lives.

About a quarter of all households are single person households compared to just one-eighth in 1961. Fourteen per cent of all families with dependent children are single parents compared to just eight per cent in 1971 (*Social Trends, 1990*).

Between 1901 and 1987 the number of people aged over 65 in Britain increased from 1.7 million to almost nine million. Of these, 5.3 million are women and 3.5 million are men. By 1996 it is expected that the number of people over the age of 65 will rise to 9.2 million. The most significant increase is among people aged over 75 years, the majority of whom are women (*Social Trends, 1990*).

Social and demographic changes make it increasingly likely that less households will conform to the nuclear family model in the future. However, despite such changes, the assumptions about families and women's role continue: households such as single people and single parents are viewed as transitional or residual stages in peoples' lives. Gay and lesbian couples are not generally viewed as 'real couples'.

Lack of child-care facilities

Research shows that a major constraint on employment opportunities for women who are mothers is the lack of child-care facilities. In the United Kingdom public child-care facilities are provided for less than two per cent of children under three and less than one per cent of children at primary school

(*Family Policy Studies Centre, 1989*). Also there are less than half the nursery places available than there were in 1945.

Some employers are recognising the need for the provision of child-care facilities at work, or payments for private child-minding, in order to encourage women back to work. However, these increases in child-care provision are likely to be short-term in nature to cope with the acute shortage of labour in the 1990s and such provision is likely to be cut back when the need for women workers diminishes.

It is generally believed that child-care is not the responsibility of the government or employers and the burden of caring for children continues to fall largely to women at home. Married women with children often have to accept the most exploitative forms of work such as casual, temporary, part-time and home-working which fit in with their domestic and child-care responsibilities.

Women and 'community care'

Government proposals for care in the community, due to be introduced in April 1991, are likely to have far-reaching consequences for women who form the largest proportion of carers and also the largest proportion of people needing care and support themselves (*Local Government Information Unit, 1990*).

The Government's White Paper, *Caring For People*, places heavy emphasis on future delivery of care services by private and voluntary agencies rather than local authorities. Under the terms of the paper, councils are encouraged to close homes for older people and cut services such as meals on wheels,

Imogen Young/FORMAT

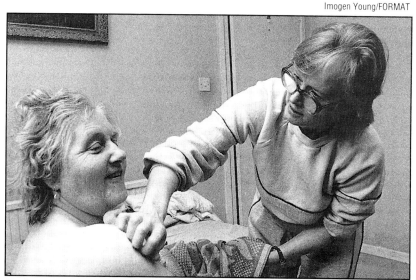

The Government proposals for 'care in the community' mean more unpaid work for women. Most carers are women and most people being cared for are women.

transport for disabled people and home-helps.

The theory behind the Government's proposals is that people who need support will be cared for by a combination of professionals, family, friends and neighbours, either in their own homes or the home of a relative. However, research conducted by the Carers National Association in 1988 found that 83% of carers receive no help at all, either from family, friends or professionals (*Local Government Information Unit, 1990*).

Today, one adult in seven in Britain cares for children, older or disabled relatives at home. Overall about 15% of women are carers (and 12% of men). Women not only form a higher proportion of carers but also tend to spend longer periods than men caring for dependents: 64% of female carers spend at least 20 hours per week caring for dependents at home compared to just 36% of men (*Family Policy Studies Centre, 1989*).

When women take on an unpaid caring role, their access to paid employment is severely curtailed. The Government proposals for 'care in the community' mean that more women may have to combine unpaid caring at home with poorly paid work outside the home or rely on male partners for partial or full financial support.

The White Paper also contains nothing about the standards that people using care and support services can expect or how the quality of these services can be monitored. It is particularly worrying that the White Paper has nothing to say about housing provision for disabled and older people. What does seem clear is that cuts in public care and support services mean disabled and older women will be less able to live independently in their own homes, unless they can afford to pay for private services and adaptations. Because of their low incomes, most women who need care and support are bound to lose out.

Social security: who benefits?

The social security system has traditionally been based on the notion of the nuclear family. Women who live with male partners are still denied access to many benefits and resources in their own right on the assumption that their needs are met within the family.

Under current benefit rules, the income of a married or cohabiting couple is aggregated and income support, housing benefit and other benefits are paid to the nominated household 'head' (normally the man). At the same time, relationships between lesbians and gays are not even officially recognised – lesbian and gay couples are always treated as single people for the purpose of benefit calculation.

Age-related changes in social security

Young people have been particularly hard hit by recent changes in social security legislation. The 1986 Social Security Act introduced age-related benefits which meant young people aged under 25 received lower rates of benefit. The assumption behind the legislation is that young people under the age of 25 are likely to be living with parents and, therefore, have lower outgoings than most older people.

In September 1988 income support was withdrawn for nearly all 16-17 year olds. In general, only young people who are not required to register for employment retain the right to claim. This includes single parents and young women who are six months pregnant or more. Many young people are not able, or do not wish, to live at home. This legislation takes away their right to independent living.

Single payments, out – social fund, in

The 1986 Social Security Act abolished the system of single payments from the DHSS (now the DSS) and replaced this with a system of loans and grants from a 'social fund'. This means that people no longer receive emergency payments for household and other essential items, such as furniture, which are not covered by income support payments.

Furthermore, the replacement of urgent needs payments with crisis loans for rent in advance, and the withdrawal of payments for deposits, means that many women with low incomes cannot get access to private rented housing.

The way that the social fund currently operates means that payment is at the discretion of local officers. Preliminary research aimed at monitoring the effects of the social fund, between July 1988 and February 1989, showed increasing numbers of people were referred to social workers because of social fund problems. Most of these referrals – about 54% – were women (*Saul Becker, July 1989*).

The introduction of the social fund particularly affects women leaving relationships who no longer receive automatic help where needed in setting up their own home. It means that many women with little or no independent source of income may be forced to stay for longer periods in unsuitable housing conditions.

Cuts in income for disabled and older women

The 1986 Social Security Act abolished additional payments for heating and personal care (such as extra baths, clothing and laundry allowances) which were available to disabled and older people. Many disabled and older women faced huge drops in their weekly benefit allowance as a result. The changes made it increasingly difficult for disabled people and older people to live independently (see *Jenny Morris, 1988*).

Changes in board and lodgings payments

Changes in legislation which came into effect in April and October 1989 mean that social security claimants no longer receive board and lodgings payments from the DSS. Instead, they must claim income support and also housing benefit from local authorities. This has resulted in the loss of 'eating out allowances', long delays in payments and less money due to cuts in housing benefit.

The Women's Aid Federation England (WAFE) say that women escaping violence are among those who have been hard hit by the changes in board and lodgings regulations. WAFE estimate that the income of women in refuges has been cut by between £20 and £40 a week. Many refuges are dependent for most of their income on the regular fixed rents which were received from the DSS. Now, refuges have to charge 'market rents' and hope that women's housing benefit will cover the cost. WAFE say that many low-funded refuges now face closure.

Changes in taxation

Until this year, a married woman's income was assumed to be her husband's for tax purposes. In the budget of March 1990, independent taxation was introduced and the aggregation rule was abolished. However, the married couple's tax allowance which replaced the married man's allowance is still received by the husband unless his earnings are insufficient to use it. The Equal Opportunities Commission points out that this means married women continue to take home less pay than married men in the same circumstances (*EOC, 1989*).

The poll tax

Because of their low incomes, women are disproportionately losing out since the introduction of the poll tax. The poll tax, or community charge, was introduced in April 1990 and replaced the old general rates system. The poll tax is paid by every adult member of every household unless they are exempt from the charge (such as residents of hospitals or residential care homes, residents of short-term hostels, people with 'no fixed abode' and persons with severe mental impairment).

In practice, many married women were not directly responsible for paying rates under the old system. It is paradoxical that, while married and cohabiting women are not entitled to welfare benefits in their own right, they are simultaneously now faced with personally addressed poll tax bills. Women who have no income of their own are now increasingly dependent on husbands or male partners.

People's petition against the poll tax organised by the Child Poverty Action Group.

25

Jan Pahl's research in Scotland, where the poll tax was introduced last year, shows that women are meeting their community charge by deducting money from their housekeeping, thereby reducing the amount available for family budgets and themselves (*Jan Pahl, 1990*).

Under the new system, divorced and separated women could be held liable for arrears of their own and also their partner's poll tax even though they have little income of their own.

Care agencies point out that the poll tax will act as a disincentive to caring for relatives at home and is, in effect, a tax on community care. At the same time, spending cuts to lower poll tax bills will inevitably reduce the quality and supply of care services.

Women in privately rented accommodation will also lose out because it is unlikely that rents inclusive of rates will be adjusted. Young women at home, single women and single parents already experiencing hardship because of their low incomes will be further disadvantaged because of the poll tax. Women also make up the vast majority of nursing and residential care workers, many of whom used to pay rates as part of their total rent, but who now will have to pay the poll tax on top of this.

Conclusion

There is ample research to show that, in general, women are poorer than men. Working women are largely confined to low-paid, low-status employment. Social policies have always been based on the 'nuclear family' model and have never provided women as individuals with an adequate 'safety net'. Today, social and demographic changes, such as greater longevity and increasing divorce and separation, mean even less women fit the assumptions on which such policies have been based.

The erosion of welfare rights through recent changes in legislation means that women are losing out even more. Policy makers can no longer ignore women's right to independent access to income, housing and other resources ■

chapter two

WOMEN'S HOUSING OPTIONS

This chapter looks at women's access to different housing tenures and shows how they face disadvantage in every sector of the housing market. The chapter also looks at how different groups of women are disadvantaged in access to housing and shows how this disadvantage continues at each stage in women's lives.

Women as home-owners

During the 1970s owner-occupation became the majority tenure in Britain with 52% of all households owning or buying their own homes by 1979. Home-ownership continued to rise in the 1980s, so that by 1989, 66% of households owned or were buying their homes (*Housing and Construction Statistics, 1989*). Following current trends, it seems likely that the proportion of home-owners in Britain today will continue to rise in the 1990s.

The advantages of home-buying are well known: relative security of tenure and investment for old age. Owning your own home also provides control and freedom from restrictions on use and alterations. However, the other side of the coin is that owner-occupation often means difficulties with paying a mortgage and high expenditure on repairs and maintenance. Home-buying can end up being a liability rather than a form of investment and security.

As the diagram on page 28 shows, a far higher proportion (73%) of married couples are buying or own their own homes than any category of unmarried men or women.

Many married couples will be dual-income families which makes home-ownership an affordable option. However, the diagram also shows that, in all the non-married adult categories, men are more likely than women to own or be buying their homes. This suggests that women, more than men, rely on a second wage to become home-owners.

Research by the National Child Development Study confirmed that cohabiting or married 23-year old women were over 100 times more likely to be owners than single women. For men, however, being married had no direct effect on tenure. Further analysis of income and job security confirmed that women generally have to rely on their partner's income and employment to become home-owners. (*Moira Munro and Susan Smith, 1989*, quoted in *Jenny Morris and M. Winn, 1990*).

Figure 1

Home-owners by sex and marital status
(as a percentage of each category)

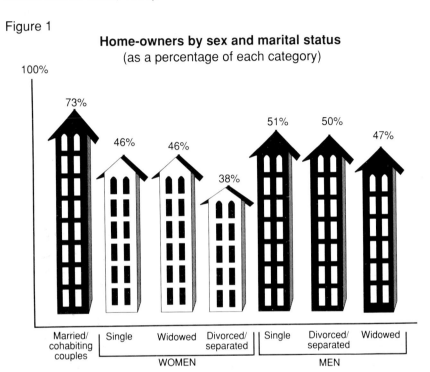

Source: General Household Survey, 1987, Table 3.24 (b), p.114 (HMSO, 1989).

Figure 1 also shows that a comparatively high proportion of widowed women own their homes (46%). Many of these widows are older women who have inherited the properties from their husbands and often face particular difficulties as home-owners due to their low incomes.

Research shows that when women do own their homes they generally lose out, in comparison to men, again because of their low incomes. Research by the Nationwide Anglia Building Society shows that, nationally, women generally buy cheaper properties than men, such as flats and terraced houses, rather than detached and semi-detached houses. Women also commit more of their income to mortgage repayments than men (*Nationwide Anglia Building Society Report, 1989*).

28

Women as council tenants

As home-ownership rose in the 1980s, there was a dramatic fall in the number of people renting council houses from 31% in 1981 to 24% in 1989 (*Housing and Construction Statistics, September 1989*). This is largely due to a fall in the number of council houses available for rent because of the introduction of the right-to-buy in 1980 and a fall in the number of new council houses built due to reduced public investment (see chapter five).

Figure 2

Council tenants by sex and marital status
(as a percentage of each category)

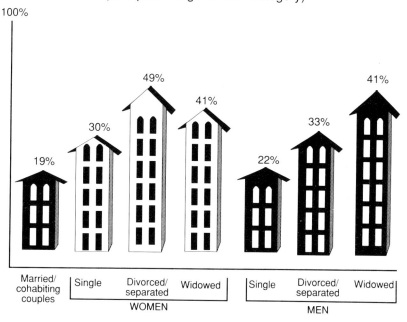

Source: General Household Survey, 1987, Table 3.24 (b) p.114 (HMSO, 1989).

In general, council tenants have always been low-income households in comparison to home-owners. In the 1990s, people with low incomes continue to rely on council housing because home-buying is not a realistic option.

Because of their low incomes, more women rely on council housing than men. As the table above shows, in each of the single adult categories, women are more likely to be council tenants than men in a similar position. In particular, more divorced and separated women rely on the council sector for housing (49% compared to just 33% of men in similar circumstances). Significantly,

29

woman-headed households are twice as likely as male-headed households to be council tenants (42% compared to 21%).

Interestingly, a lower proportion of married couples are council tenants than any other group. Despite this, the policies behind public housing provision are geared towards 'family' housing, by which local authorities mean conventional, heterosexual, two-parent family accommodation. Single people, single parents and lesbian and gay couples can face discrimination in access to suitable housing (see, for example, Mary Braily, 1982).

In chapter five, the decline in public provision of housing is examined showing that this has a detrimental effect on women.

Women as private tenants

The 1980s saw the continuation of a long-term decline in the private rented sector so that, by 1989, just seven per cent of households rented privately compared to 15% in 1971. Traditionally, the private rented sector has provided homes for many people who cannot afford, or do not wish, to own their homes. Today it remains an important source of accommodation for certain groups of people, particularly older people and young people.

The English House Condition Survey (1986) found a high proportion of privately rented dwellings – 42% – in poor condition (compared to 13% of owner-occupied dwellings, 11% of council homes and seven per cent of housing association dwellings).

In the private rented sector, tenants can face high rents and insecurity of tenure, particularly since the 1988 Housing Act, which made it possible for landlords to charge market rents and reduced tenants' security of tenure (see chapter five).

Women who are private tenants also face the additional problem of sexual harassment and abuse from landlords and other tenants. Black women face both racial and sexual harassment and abuse. Private renting is, therefore, not always an attractive source of accommodation for women. Nevertheless, some women, particularly single women (18% of whom are private tenants), have to remain in this sector because they have no other housing options.

Women and housing associations

Between 1976 and 1988, the number of housing association dwellings increased by 86%. However, housing associations still account for less than three per cent of Britain's housing stock (Housing and Construction Statistics, 1989).

Housing associations have traditionally been a source of housing for people on low incomes who have difficulty obtaining housing in other sectors.

However, housing associations have been hit hard by recent housing legislation and their role as providers of affordable, decent housing for those in need is in danger of being undermined (this issue is discussed further in chapter five).

Young Women: leaving home, living where?

Catherine, a young Irish woman, came to England after leaving home because of family stress. She was unable to find accommodation, could not get a place on a YTS scheme and received no income support, only a £15 bridging allowance. Eventually she went to a night shelter because she had no money, no friends or relatives to help with accommodation and nowhere else to go.

About three-quarters of all young people have moved away from home by the age of 23 (*National Child Development Study*, quoted in *Alex Cosgrave, 1988*). However, young people are disadvantaged in the housing market because they generally earn low incomes in comparison to older people. As a consequence, their options for setting up home independently are usually extremely limited. Research shows that nearly half of all young people leave home to get married or live with a partner (*Alex Cosgrave, 1988*).

A major problem for young people leaving home is their lower incomes in comparison to older people. A survey by MORI in 1987 showed that 84% of young people aged 15-26 saw independent living as a big financial problem. About 30% of those interviewed who were still living at home said that they had to live with their parents because they could not afford to leave.

Because of their low incomes, few young women are able to become home-owners in their own right. Cutbacks in the supply of council housing over the past decade means that young people have less access to public housing. Because housing policies are geared towards 'families', single young people face the same barriers as single older people in getting accommodation in the council sector.

Because of a lack of other options, private renting continues to be an important source of housing for young people. About 38% of households in privately rented furnished accommodation have household heads aged under 25 (*General Household Survey, 1987, p.113*). Young people have been particularly disadvantaged by the 1988 Housing Act which has made it easier for landlords to charge whatever rents they wish (see chapter five).

Housing providers and policy makers generally assume that young women (and young men) will wish to, and be able to, stay in the parental home until they form a permanent relationship and move away to set up their own home.

However, this is not always what women want, or are able, to do.

Many young people cannot continue to live at home because of things like overcrowding, family arguments, poverty, abuse and harassment. A recent pilot study conducted by Centrepoint, an organisation in London who provide accommodation for young homeless people, showed that the parental home had been the last home of less than half of those interviewed at a night shelter (49 were interviewed in total). Forty-one per cent of those interviewed had been in care at some time in the past two years.

Four-fifths of young people interviewed by Centrepoint had had to leave home because of 'push' factors, such as eviction, family arguments or being asked to leave. Two-thirds said that they could not return to their last home even if they had nowhere else to go (*Geoffrey Randall, 1989*).

Recent changes in benefit entitlement, introducing age-related benefits, withdrawing entitlement for 16 and 17-year olds and making local authorities responsible for board and lodgings payments, further disadvantage young women in the housing market. As it was pointed out in chapter two, these changes take away the right of young people to live independently.

The National Association of Citizens Advice Bureaux (NACAB) have found many young women have been adversely affected by benefit entitlement changes. A Citizens Advice Bureau (CAB) in West London reported a case where a 16 year old woman illegally lost her job when she became pregnant. She was unable to find further work and was ineligible for income support. She contacted the CAB when her mother threatened to evict her.

A Wolverhampton CAB reported a case of a pregnant 16 year old who was homeless and sleeping rough. She was unable to return home, after persistent arguments with her parents. She had been refused income support and had no money at all.

Shelter estimates that about 156,000 young people experience homelessness each year. There is evidence that a high percentage of these are young women (see chapter four).

As the housing crisis continues, young women continue to experience acute difficulties in getting decent, affordable housing. Inevitably, more and more young women are forced to stay in unsuitable housing conditions because there is nowhere else for them to go.

Single women: numbers up, needs ignored

Increasingly, people in Britain are choosing to live alone. This trend has been encouraged by demographic changes such as later marriages, increasing numbers of divorces and separations and greater longevity.

Between 1971 and 1981 there was a 30% increase in the number of single person households (from 3.3 million in 1971 to 4.7 million in 1981). By 1988 a quarter of all households were single person households (*Social Trends, 1989*).

Margaret is a single woman in her early forties. She lives in a flat which she is buying with a mortgage. She likes living on her own and says it gives her a feeling of independence. But she says it has taken her years to be able to afford her own home. She spent many unhappy years in poor quality, expensive private rented accommodation because she could not afford to buy a home, and as a single woman, she did not think she would be able to get a council house in reasonable condition. Now, with a good job and reasonable security, Margaret has her own home. She is one of the lucky ones.

Researchers say that, despite the increasing trend towards living alone, the housing needs of single women have been, and continue to be, ignored or marginalised by housing providers and policy makers (see *Sophie Watson and Helen Austerberry, 1986*).

Single women (and single men) are virtually excluded from access to local authority housing unless they fall into one of the 'vulnerable' categories under Part III of the 1985 Housing Act, for example, as a result of old age, mental or physical disability.

In 1985, CHAR, the campaign for single homeless people, conducted a survey of allocation policies in over 400 housing authorities in England and Wales. Three hundred and two authorities completed and returned the questionnaire. Of these, 80% were found to be operating restrictions in their allocations policy which limited single people from registering on waiting lists, including minimum age limits (36%) and minimum residence requirements (74%). Only six per cent of the authorities who returned the questionnaire allowed single people access to council housing by implementing policies which extended the provisions of Part III of the 1985 Housing Act (*Sheila Venn, 1985*).

More single men than single women own their own homes (51% compared to 46% – see diagram on page 28). Because of their low incomes, women are currently losing out in the home-buying market. The Nationwide Anglia Building Society point out that the average income of women borrowers has risen by less than that of men – 157% compared to 173% . As a result, the real cost (i.e. the ratio of house prices to income) has increased more sharply for women than for men. Women borrowers are therefore likely to find it increasingly difficult to become home-owners in the future.

Relationship breakdown: where do women go?

> June recently split up with her husband and was left on her own with one small son. She works part-time as a care assistant earning very low wages.
>
> June had taken out a joint mortgage with her husband and their home is now up for sale. June, therefore, has to move. She would like to buy a home but cannot afford it, so she has applied to the council for accommodation. Although June will almost certainly qualify for rehousing because she is caring for a small child, she has not heard yet and is desperately worried. She says *'when the house is sold I'll have nowhere to go. I could be on the streets...'*

It was pointed out earlier that policy makers and popular perceptions see the family as a nuclear unit, in which all members benefit equally. However, policies constructed around such perceptions do not make allowances for what happens when the family unit breaks down and the disadvantage some members of the unit face in obtaining individual access to income, housing and other resources (*Frances Logan, 1986*).

Women who have been financially dependent, whether partially or fully, on male partners for long periods will experience acute disadvantage in the housing market on divorce and separation. Unless the assets received from a relationship are high or she can retain her home in her own right, a woman experiencing relationship breakdown is likely to suffer great hardship in attempting to get rehoused or avoid homelessness.

For example, on divorce, courts are awarded extensive powers to deal with ownership of matrimonial homes. However, it is universal practice for courts to consider first the housing needs of any dependent children. So, women get housing for themselves mainly in their role as mothers. In some cases, courts have made orders that the home be sold when the children reach 18, making women homeless at a time when they have no 'priority need' for council accommodation under the law and are unlikely to be able to buy their own homes.

Even when women are able to retain their homes, unless their prospects for future employment are good, many lenders will not be prepared to continue lending for the mortgage (*Frances Logan, 1986*).

Just 38% of separated or divorced women are home-owners compared to 50% of men in similar circumstances (see Fig. 1, p.28). This serves as an indicator of the disadvantage women face when relationships break down and the fact that many women will move out of the owner-occupied sector on the break-up of a relationship because they cannot afford to keep up mortgage repayments alone.

More divorced and separated women rely on the council sector than men (49% compared to 33% – see the diagram on page 29). This is particularly the case when a woman has been financially dependent and has no income or savings in her own right.

While women remain poorer than men and, wholly or partially, financially dependent on male partners within a relationship, they will continue to experience hardship on the break-up of that relationship.

Single parents: the forgotten families

Beth, aged 46, is a single parent with many emotional problems following a very traumatic and disturbing divorce. She has two teenage daughters. The eldest, aged 18 and the youngest, aged 16, are mentally and emotionally disturbed. Care and Repair, the agency Beth contacted say, *'Our client is very much in need of assistance as she cannot cope alone.'* Among Beth's problems are substantial repairs which are required to her home.

About 15% of all families with dependent children are headed by a lone parent and about 90% of lone parents are women (*General Household Survey, 1987*). This largely reflects the rise in divorce and separations: over one in two new marriages is likely to end in divorce and two-thirds of lone mothers are divorced or separated (*Social Trends, 1990*).

The Finer Report (1974) found that one-parent families were likely to be poorer than two-parent families and living in worse housing conditions. Single parents were found to be less likely to own their own homes and more likely to be council tenants or private tenants than other households.

Today, the picture for single parents has not changed much. The income of lone parents is about 40% that of two-parent families. An estimated 55% rely on benefits compared to only seven per cent of two-parent families. Over twice as many two-parent families own their own homes as single parents. Conversely, over twice as many single parents as two-parent families are council tenants (*Radience Strathdee, 1989*).

A major constraint on lone parents' access to decent and affordable housing is the disadvantage they face in access to employment. The Women's National Commission (1989) set up a working party to look at the barriers lone parents face in combining paid work and child-care responsibilities. These barriers included disincentives within the benefit system (primarily, that no account is taken of child-care expenses in income support benefit calculations), the lack of good quality and affordable child-care facilities (see chapter one) and the current employment structures which do not allow for flexible working arrangements. At the same time, women who obtain part-time work do not enjoy the same employment rights and security as full-time workers.

The Women's National Commission recommended that the DSS should consider including reasonable work-related expenses in income support entitlement. They also recommended that the Government should consider making lone parents exempt from taxation on child-care costs and that child-care should be a priority issue.

Concerning employment, the Women's National Commission recommended that the Government should encourage employers to maximise the opportunities for part-time work as well as maximising the use of flexible working arrangements. The Commission also said that the Department of Employment should consider the extension of employment rights to part-time workers.

In recent years, policy makers have demonstrated a preoccupation with the growth in single parents and made the assumption that the growth in teenage pregnancies is the result of priority treatment in access to public housing. John Moore, the former Secretary of State for Social Security, has referred in a number of speeches to a young, unmarried woman in his constituency who told him she intended to get pregnant in order to jump the housing waiting list.

Mrs Thatcher was reported in an interview in *The Times* (26/10/88) as being anxious to act on the '*growing problem in the Welfare State of young single girls who deliberately become pregnant in order to jump a housing queue and gain welfare benefits*' (quoted in *Jonathan Bradshaw, 1989, p.5*).

The National Council for One Parent Families recently commissioned a research project to test the assumption about teenage pregnancies and access to council housing. The study showed that housing was rarely considered at all by young pregnant women. None of the 38 women interviewed saw motherhood as a passport to guaranteed housing or income. Most said they had little knowledge of housing or income matters when they became pregnant. Lack of money was the biggest problem for all the young women interviewed (*Emma Clarke, 1989*).

Added to this is the fact that unmarried mothers today account for just a third of single parent families – two-thirds are the result of marriage break-up. Also, despite the Government's preoccupation with teenage pregnancies, statistics indicate that only a minority of unmarried mothers are teenagers and 51% of all unmarried mothers are aged over 24 (*General Household Survey, 1987*).

So the problem to be addressed by policy makers should be the disadvantage women face on the breakdown of heterosexual relationships, which mean they have to rely on state benefits and public housing, rather than young women deliberately getting pregnant.

Older women: who cares?

Ethel, aged 77, lives alone in a large four-bedroomed house. She suffers from chronic chest complaints and has impaired hearing. Ethel lives on a state pension and a small pension from her late husband which takes her above the income support level.

Ethel's house is desperately in need of repairs. Water is leaking from the tank and gutters through her living room ceiling which is now in a dangerous condition. Ethel does not know who to turn to for help.

The population of Britain is gradually ageing. Over the last decade, the proportion of women aged over 75 has increased from six per cent of the total population in 1977 to eight per cent in 1987, while the proportion of men aged over 75 has increased from three per cent in 1977 to four per cent in 1987. It is anticipated that future increases in the size of the older population will be mainly among the very old, aged over 88, for whom a massive increase of 74% by the year 2005 is forecast (*General Household Surveys, 1986/7*).

About 95% of older people live in conventional housing. Agencies working with older people say that the majority wish to stay in their own homes, given adequate support services, and most have only limited options for moving away (see, for example, *Care and Repair, Annual Report, 1989*).

The English House Condition Survey (1986) showed that persons aged over 75 were more likely than other people to occupy housing which was unfit or lacked basic amenities, occupying almost a third of dwellings lacking basic amenities and 16% of unfit dwellings.

Older persons living alone were also found to be more likely to occupy housing in poor condition than older couples (19% compared to 14%). Most older persons living alone are women due to women's greater longevity.

About 52% of tenants living in privately rented accommodation are aged over 65 or over (*General Household Survey, 1986*). Many of these are older women living alone. Under the 1988 Housing Act, local authorities lost their power to register 'fair rents' in the private sector (see chapter five). This had acted to protect tenants such as older women who may be frail and vulnerable to such harassment. Many women are now increasingly vulnerable to harassment by landlords who want to sell their properties or rent them to better-off tenants.

As the English House Condition Survey (1986) showed, conditions in the private rented sector are worse than in any other housing sector. Today, many older women are forced to remain in private rented accommodation, with little or no legal rights, because of a lack of housing options.

Renting by people of pensionable age in the council sector has increased over the past decade, from 31% in 1981 to 39% in 1987 (*General Household Survey, 1987*). Older people, among which women are disproportionately represented, are increasingly losing out as public sector provision of housing declines (see chapter five).

The provision of sheltered housing often ignores the needs and wishes of older people. For example, older people may want some choice about who they live with. Black and ethnic minority women and lesbians may wish to live with other women with similar life styles. There is a need for sheltered housing provision to be based around the needs and experiences of older people.

Agencies working with older women have found that one of the main problems is that older women lack information about the range of housing and support services which are open to them. In the absence of such information, many older women are left in totally unsuitable housing.

Local authorities, housing associations and related agencies and organisations must begin to tailor their policies towards the needs and wishes of older people, and particular groups of older people.

Disabled women: homes fit to live in?

Josie is registered disabled and has difficulty getting up stairs. She used to live in council accommodation but was evicted for rent arrears. She is now living in a privately rented flat on the third floor. Her living conditions are poor and she has no hot water and has to go next door to have a bath or shower. She lives with a partner who is verbally abusive and who takes most of her money from her.

There are currently over six million adults in Britain – one in ten – who have one or more disabilities. All research indicates that more women than men are disabled, partly because of the over-representation of older people among disabled persons. The Office of Population Censuses and Surveys (OPCS) study in 1988 showed that almost 70% of disabled adults were aged 60 or over.

Disabled people are generally poorer than able-bodied people. The OPCS Survey found that disabled adults were half as likely as able-bodied adults to be working. Disabled people who were working were found to be earning less than able-bodied people. Three-quarters of disabled adults relied on state benefits as their main source of income.

Because of their low incomes, disabled women often experience acute disadvantage in access to suitable housing. Also, the provision of housing across all tenures generally ignores the physical requirements of disabled people (*Jenny Morris, 1990*).

As home-owners, disabled people are more likely than other households to experience poor housing conditions. This is because of the association between old age and low income, and also because of the association between disability and low income (*Jenny Morris, 1990*).

One in two disabled persons lives in council housing compared to one in four of all households. This is partly because disabled people are more likely than able-bodied people to be on low incomes and, therefore, relying on the council sector for accommodation. Also, most housing which is purpose built or adapted for disabled people is owned by local authorities (*Jenny Morris, 1990*).

However, recent research shows that local authorities appear to have very limited information about their disabled tenants. Jenny Morris contacted 21 housing departments in Britain and found that there was little or no knowledge among the authorities about the demand for housing among disabled people or what, if any, appropriate housing provision existed in their areas (*Jenny Morris, 1990*).

As the council stock is depleted, through right-to-buy sales and privatisation, what is left is the poorer quality stock which has less potential for adaptation. Disabled people, more of whom are women, are therefore increasingly losing out. More and more are forced to live in totally unsuitable housing conditions.

Most disabled people are able, and would wish to, live in their own homes, provided the necessary support and/or adaptations are available. However, many disabled people are currently not able to do this. Research carried out by the Royal College of Physicians in 1985 showed that over half of all the disabled people under retirement age in Britain who are in residential care are in inappropriate places (quoted in *Jenny Morris, 1988*).

The lack of suitable accommodation for disabled people today means many disabled women continue to have little choice about how or where they live.

Lesbians: no provision

Juliet and Rachel shared a home in Leeds. For over a year they were continually harassed by a neighbour because of their lesbian relationship and were eventually forced to move out. The harassment started with verbal abuse and went on to physical assault. Eventually, Juliet and Rachel sold their house and moved away, but it meant that they had to move into a more expensive house and they both had difficulty paying the new mortgage on their low incomes.

Gay and lesbian groups estimate that about one in ten people in Britain is a lesbian or gay man. However, housing provision in Britain is geared to conventional heterosexual family units in both the public and private sector. Also, researchers, housing providers and policy makers do not generally collect statistics on lesbians and gay men or their particular needs and experiences in the housing market.

In general, both policy makers and housing providers ignore lesbians and gays in respect of housing. Lesbian and gay couples do not have any rights of succession to local authority properties or private rented accommodation on the death of a partner and they have no statutory right to accommodation on the breakdown of relationships.

Councils do not generally accept harassment on the grounds of sexuality as grounds for leaving home, so lesbians leaving violent situations are in danger of being classed as intentionally homeless and refused accommodation.

Lesbians and gay men generally stay single longer than heterosexual couples, so are less likely to be able to afford their own homes. Also, lesbian and gay couples frequently face discrimination by building societies when they apply for mortgages because it is assumed that their relationships are not as permanent as heterosexual relationships (*CHAR, 1988*).

At a recent national conference about the housing needs of lesbians and gays, particular issues identified by women were, harassment and discrimination, homelessness, especially when lesbians and gays 'come out' to friends, parents and other relatives, and the lack of temporary accommodation for lesbians and gays (*CHAR, 1989*).

The lack of research on the needs and experiences of lesbians and gays in the housing market means that their particular problems of access to suitable housing remain hidden from public view. It is essential that researchers, policy makers and housing providers begin to take these needs and experiences seriously.

Women in rural areas

Women living in rural areas of Britain often experience different problems to those of women in urban and inner-city areas. However, the issue of how women can get access to suitable housing remains the same.

In rural areas, housing and employment are often in short supply, so women have little chance of becoming home-owners. In areas which are popular with tourists, women can find work, at least during the tourist season, in the service industry as cleaners, chambermaids, cooks and waitresses. However, the pay is notoriously low. Also, accommodation in the private rented sector is almost non-existent in such areas because landlords prefer to rent to tourists whom they can charge higher rents.

Women escaping violence have problems because there is less temporary and emergency housing provision and often inadequate transport.

Many former council tenants have bought their homes in rural areas, since the 1980 Housing Act introduced the right-to-buy, because properties are often well-kept and include popular semi-detached houses with gardens. Although enabling some people to become home-owners, this has led to a drastic reduction in council housing in many rural areas, exacerbating the problems of women looking for accommodation.

Conclusion

This chapter has shown that women often have less choice in the housing market than men. Furthermore, the housing system operates to the disadvantage of particular groups of women, including disabled women, lesbians, single parents, single women, older women and young women. Given women's disadvantaged position in the housing market, it is essential that policy makers begin to recognise women's need for independent access to suitable and affordable housing ■

chapter three

BLACK AND ETHNIC MINORITY WOMEN'S HOUSING

Sushila, an Asian woman in her mid-forties, moved to London recently after persistent racial harassment by neighbours in the West Midlands. She is staying with friends at the moment and wants to start a new life. She now feels that she has outstayed her welcome and cannot impose on her friends any longer.

Jena, a young Filipino woman, came to Britain to work. She obtained privately rented accommodation, and had to take on two jobs in order to pay her rent. Jena went to her local council to ask for a council house because her rent is too high and she cannot find any cheaper accommodation. The council officer she spoke to told her she should return to the Phillipines.

Traditionally, the housing needs and experiences of black and ethnic minority women in Britain have been ignored or marginalised. This chapter hopes to go some way towards rectifying this by focusing on black and ethnic minority women's housing in Britain today.

Lack of information

Researchers, policy makers and housing providers rarely break down their statistics both by gender and ethnic origin, so the particular discrimination and disadvantage that black and ethnic minority women face in the housing market is largely hidden from view.

Furthermore, there is often little or no consultation between ethnic minority communities and public or voluntary agencies regarding housing needs and related policy issues.

The combination of discrimination, lack of statistical information and inadequate consultation has led to a lack of housing policies which are responsive to the needs of black and ethnic minority households.

Poor housing conditions

A major national survey by the Policy Studies Institute in the early 1980s showed that the housing circumstances of black and ethnic minority households in Britain are, in many ways, inferior to those of white households.

Overall, Asian and West Indian households were found to occupy property which is less desirable than properties occupied by white households. Among owner-occupiers and council tenants, more black and ethnic minority households were found to live in older properties. They were also less likely to live in detached and semi-detached houses than white households (*Colin Brown, 1984*).

Discrimination in the council sector

Many researchers have shown how black and ethnic minority men and women are discriminated against in the council sector in terms of access to housing (see, for example, reports by the *Commission for Racial Equality (CRE), 1988, Alan Simpson, 1981*).

At a recent conference about black and ethnic minority women and housing held in the London Borough of Lambeth, women talked in workshops about how they face particular disadvantage and discrimination in access to council housing due to the combination of sexism and racism.

Recent research conducted in the London boroughs of Wandsworth and Southwark (*Nirmala Rao, 1990*) shows that black and ethnic minority women face discrimination in access to council housing compared to white women. The study showed that black and ethnic minority women tend to wait for longer periods before being housed and tend to be allocated poorer quality properties than white women.

The study also showed that twice as many white women as black and ethnic minority women live in semi-detached or terraced houses (75% compared to 62%), and that more black and ethnic minority women live in flats (24% compared to 11%). Nearly two-thirds of the black and ethnic minority women in the study living in flats were in high rise blocks, above the fifth floor, compared to just one-third of white women.

Also, 90% of black and ethnic minority women with three or more children were found to be living in one-bedroomed flats or maisonettes (compared to just 65% of white women). Seventeen per cent of white women with three or more children lived in terraced properties compared to just nine per cent of black and ethnic minority women (*Nirmala Rao, 1990*).

Discrimination in the private rented sector

Black and ethnic minority women often have to rent in the private sector because they face discrimination in access to decent council housing and cannot afford to own their homes. About nine per cent of all households in private rented accommodation are occupied by black and ethnic minority households (*Ealing Council and FBHO, 1989*). Yet in the private rented sector they face poor conditions and overcrowding as well as harassment and discrimination.

A survey by the Greater London Council (GLC) of private tenants in London in 1983/4 showed that over 30% of black and ethnic minority households in the privately rented sector either lack or share basic amenities (compared to 15% of white households). More black and ethnic minority households were found to be living in overcrowded and poor housing conditions. They were also more likely to be paying higher rents than white households (*GLC, 1986*).

The GLC Survey found that only 42% of black and ethnic minority households were in protected tenancies compared to 66% of white households. Also, 11% of black and ethnic minority households had experienced harassment by landlords compared to just four per cent of white households.

The 1982 Policy Studies Institute (PSI) survey showed that, nationally, black and ethnic minority private tenants have less basic facilities, more overcrowding and less detached and semi-detached housing than white tenants (*Colin Brown, 1984*).

Following the 1988 Housing Act, which reduces the security of tenants in privately rented accommodation (see chapter five), black and ethnic minority people are likely to be more vulnerable to harassment and discrimination.

Is home-ownership the answer?

Research suggests that black and ethnic minority households can face discrimination by building societies in trying to obtain a mortgage. Research in Leeds (*L. Stevens et al, 1981*) showed that black and ethnic minority families were being indirectly discriminated against because building societies were less likely to lend in the oldest inner-city areas of Leeds where there is a large ethnic minority community. The study suggests that the failure to lend is not associated with the quality of housing stock but rather with the social and ethnic characteristics of the neighbourhood.

Research in Rochdale by the CRE (1985) also found indirect discrimination against black and ethnic minority households. The CRE found that decisions on how to lend were left to the discretion of local branch managers. Practices included not lending on a house without a front garden and not lending on cheaper range properties. The effect of this was to discriminate against black and ethnic minority households who could only afford to buy these types of properties.

The 1982 PSI Survey shows that, in all areas of Britain and across all social classes, the proportion of Asians owning their homes in Britain is higher than either whites or West Indians. On average, about 72% of all Asians own their homes in Britain. The high proportion of Asian home-owners is explained by the history of owner-occupation among Asian people. The high level of home-ownership was, in part, a response to the limited options in other forms of tenure and was characterised by the outright purchase of relatively cheap, poor quality houses. Also, the existence of support networks within the Asian community enabled families to turn to relatives and friends for help with the deposit for a mortgage (*Colin Brown, 1984*).

While many black and ethnic minority households are not able to buy their homes due to discrimination or lack of income, others are forced into owner-occupation because of the discrimination they face in access to housing in the public and private rented sectors. Many of these households live in poor conditions because of a lack of housing choices. The 1982 PSI survey found that black and ethnic minority households who own their homes are more likely than white households to live in poor and overcrowded conditions (*Colin Brown, 1984*).

Cultural differences in family size mean black and ethnic minority families often require larger houses. However, discrimination in the labour market resulting in low pay and high unemployment mean that even when home-ownership is attained, black and ethnic minority households can experience problems with mortgage payments and escalating disrepair.

Homelessness: a growing problem

Homelessness is a growing problem among black and ethnic minority communities. Research in London shows that black and ethnic minority households are up to four times as likely to become homeless as white households: a survey of 100 households accepted as homeless by London boroughs in 1988 revealed 40% of households were either African, Caribbean, Asian or Black UK (*Danny Friedman and Hal Pawson, 1989*).

However, black and ethnic minority homelessness can frequently be hidden within their own communities because fear of racially motivated violence precludes many from opting for the traditional voluntary sector hostel alternatives. A Home Office report in 1981 identified Asians to be 50 times more likely to be assaulted by white people and Africans, Caribbeans and black UK people to be 35 times more likely to be attacked than white people. In these circumstances, black and ethnic minority women who do not get access to the public housing system are likely to avoid voluntary sector temporary accommodation where possible.

Research shows that black and ethnic minority households applying as homeless can face discrimination by local authorities in their search for permanent accommodation. For example, the CRE found that Tower Hamlets authority had directly discriminated against black people both by refusing to provide them with permanent accommodation and in the way they were treated in respect of how long they waited for offers of accommodation. The research also found that black and ethnic minorities were indirectly discriminated against because they were disproportionately allocated to poor estates (*CRE, 1988*).

Immigrants are particularly vulnerable to homelessness and often reluctant to approach local authorities because they may have insecure immigration status. Research by Mandana Hendessi (1987) suggests that many migrants end up living in appalling conditions in bed and breakfast hostels or in overcrowded conditions with friends or relatives because there were no alternatives available.

Black and ethnic minority people who attempt to claim benefits can be asked to produce passports to prove their identity or immigration status. Discrimination by benefits officers means that less black and ethnic minority people claim benefits. This, in turn, means they are disadvantaged in access to suitable housing in all sectors.

Immigration policies and homelessness

Immigrants seeking admission to Britain may be subject to the requirement that they maintain and accommodate themselves without having 'recourse to public funds'. These 'public funds' include income support, family credit and housing benefit. They also include the housing as homeless provision of Part III of the 1985 Housing Act.

Although the maintenance requirement applies in theory to all immigrants, regardless of colour or race, black and ethnic minority women (and men) are often particularly subjected to the requirement.

The maintenance requirement means that entry clearance officers or the Home Office must be satisfied that adequate accommodation is available in Britain for the applicant and dependents. Thus black and ethnic minority women and men may not be able to exercise their right to accommodation for fear of jeopardising their immigration status.

Black and ethnic minority women and men may be asked to produce their passports either as proof of identity or to check their immigration status. However, it should be emphasised that immigration status is irrelevant to the right to apply for housing under the 1985 Housing Act except when people are in Britain illegally.

Immigrants who have left accommodation abroad may also find themselves declared 'intentionally homeless'. Black and ethnic minority people are often more likely than white people to be declared intentionally homeless because they have left accommodation abroad.

Generally, the local authority is entitled to reach this conclusion if the accommodation abroad was available for use and it was reasonable to continue to occupy it. However, in reaching their decisions, local authorities and the courts have placed too much emphasis on the decision to leave available accommodation and have not looked at factors such as the nature and adequacy of such accommodation, the desire to resettle in Britain and the need to make use of entry certificates which can take years to obtain. This narrow approach to the question of leaving accommodation appears to have found favour in the courts.

Domestic violence: where can women go?

Violence against women in the home occurs in all class, race, cultural and religious groups. However, the issue of domestic violence raises specific problems for black and ethnic minority women due to the racism and racial inequality they can face outside their own communities. Many black and ethnic minority women in Britain are forced to tolerate violence in the home because of their restricted access to income, housing and other support outside their own communities.

Black and ethnic minority women may not want to report domestic violence to the police for fear of racist treatment. For example, in the experience of Southall Black Sisters and other groups representing black and ethnic minority women, the police have used reports of domestic violence to make fishing raids for illegal immigrants, checking the passports of everyone in the household for immigration status.

There are currently about 200 or so refuges for women escaping violence

47

in Britain. About 10 of these are specifically for black and ethnic minority women. Black refuge workers say that there is a need for more refuges specifically for black and ethnic minority women.

Black and ethnic minority women may have specific needs in terms of language, diet and religious differences. These needs cannot be adequately catered for in predominantly white refuges. However, as researcher Amina Mama points out, it is racism and racial inequality, rather than cultural differences, which remain the overriding problem for black and ethnic minority women in predominately white refuges. Mama's research shows that black and ethnic minority women in predominantly white refuges face racism both from other residents and also white refuge workers (*Amina Mama, 1989*).

Racism can occur both within and outside the refuge movement and this dictates a need for refuges which are specifically for black and ethnic minority women and for more black workers within mixed and predominantly white refuges. Domestic violence is an issue for all women and in order that black and ethnic minority women receive the necessary emotional and practical support on leaving a violent relationship, racism and racial inequality must be continually challenged.

Public and voluntary services: equality for all?

Research shows that there is often a poor level of consultation and communication between statutory and voluntary services and ethnic minority communities. For example, recent research by Alison Bowes (1989) in Glasgow showed that the City Council and many voluntary agencies were not responsive to the needs of the black and ethnic minority communities.

Alison Bowes found that many Asian families in Glasgow were reluctant to use advice agencies or approach the council because they lacked Asian staff and materials in translation and, therefore, did not cater for Asian households. This resulted in many members of the ethnic minority community relying on friends and relatives for information and lacking knowledge about their housing rights.

Black and ethnic minority people who have English as a second language frequently require information and interviews to be translated. Yet this service is not usually provided.

If black and ethnic minority households lack information about the housing system, their vulnerability to exploitation is increased. There is clearly a need for more consultation between public and voluntary agencies and ethnic minority communities to ensure racial equality. Both public and voluntary agencies must also ensure that information about housing rights, including translated material, is widely and easily available.

Racial harassment and abuse

Several studies have shown how black and ethnic minority communities suffer widespread harassment and abuse both in their own homes and in contact with agencies and organisations outside, in the white community (see, for example, *CRE 1987, Lucy Bonnerjea and Jean Lawson, 1988*). Many agencies involved, including local authorities, voluntary agencies and the police, appear to have no clear policies on racial harassment or fail to implement their policies successfully.

Lucy Bonnerjea and Jean Lawton say that there is a widespread belief that racial harassment is under-reported. In addition, their research in Brent showed that where harassment was reported, the local authority took little or no action against the perpetrator (*Lucy Bonnerjea and Jean Lawton, 1988*).

Conclusion

There is a need for more research on the housing needs and experiences of black and ethnic minority women in Britain. Funding must be made available to ensure such research can be undertaken by all housing providers. In the light of research conducted so far, it is essential that local authorities, and other public and voluntary agencies and organisations begin to take these needs and experiences seriously. Policy makers should ensure that the needs of black and ethnic minority women are placed high on the agenda so that equality of opportunity can be achieved in practice ■

chapter four

WOMEN AND HOMELESSNESS: THE HIDDEN PROBLEM

Marie has three children and works part-time. She jointly owns a house with her husband. Marie's relationship with her husband began to break down a while ago. She finally left after her husband raped her.

Marie applied to her local authority for housing as a homeless person but eventually decided not to pursue her application after housing officers said it would be difficult because of the lack of evidence that she was homeless.

She has since being staying with friends and is finding it hard to secure accommodation that she can afford.

What is 'homelessness?'

The 1977 Homeless Persons Act (now Part III of the 1985 Housing Act) defined 'homelessness' by statute and placed a duty upon local authorities to assist homeless persons for the first time. However, local authorities are only obliged to house people who are homeless or who are threatened with homelessness as it is legally defined and who also have a 'priority need'. People in priority need include pregnant women, households with children and those who are 'vulnerable' because of old age, mental illness or physical disability.

Many people in need of housing can be excluded from this right to housing, including most single people and women without children, single women fleeing domestic violence and people living in sub-standard accommodation.

Shelter believes that homelessness is about more than rooflessness or the legal definition in the 1985 Housing Act. Homelessness encompasses all those in overcrowded or sub-standard or temporary accommodation, whether provided by friends, relatives, voluntary organisations or other landlords. People who feel unsafe or insecure in their accommodation, perhaps due to racial or sexual harassment, should be also regarded as homeless and given rights under the law.

Growing homelessness

Homelessness in Britain is growing. Last year 126,240 households were accepted as homeless by local authorities in England compared to just 62,930 in 1980. However, these statistics only cover people who approach local authorities for help and are accepted by local authorities for rehousing under Part III of the 1985 Housing Act. Many homeless people, particularly single people and couples without children, do not appear in local authority statistics.

Pam Isherwood/FORMAT

Young homeless women in a newly opened squat in Brixton, South London.

The Salvation Army recently estimated that there are about 75,000 visibly homeless people in London alone, including people sleeping rough, in squats and in bed and breakfast accommodation (*Salvation Army, 1989*). Official statistics, therefore, represent a gross underestimation of the problem.

Homelessness is not just a problem in big cities. At the end of 1989, 42% of households accepted as homeless by councils lived outside big towns and cities (*Joe Oldman, 1989*).

When the problem of women's homelessness is considered, official figures simply do not exist, because local authorities are not required to break down their statistics by sex. Women's homelessness is, therefore, largely hidden

51

from public view.

However, in recent years women researchers have taken on board the issue of women's homelessness and put it on the agenda for discussion. Sophie Watson and Helen Austerberry (1986) link women's homelessness to their low wages and poor employment prospects. They conclude that women often stay in inadequate housing situations because of a lack of alternatives.

Lack of emergency provision

Much research on homelessness has focused on people sleeping rough or using night shelters and hostels. However, fewer women than men fall into this category of the 'visible' homeless. One reason for this is that there is a lack of emergency provision for women with most hostels and night shelters accommodating men only.

Researchers in Bristol recently found that out of 617 bed spaces in bed and breakfast and other hostels, only 74 were for women only, while 406 were for men only (*Bristol City Council and WISH, 1988*). A recent survey in London showed that less than one in eight bedspaces in London hostels were in women-only hostels, including women's refuges. Out of a total of 8,690 bedspaces, there were 2,260 bedspaces for men. The remaining 5,190 were in mixed accommodation although, it is likely that in practice, many of these beds would not be willingly offered to women (*Tony Eardley, 1989*).

The researchers in London pointed out that the survey underestimated the number of men-only hostels because DSS resettlement units were not included in the survey and because there was a low response from some other large hostel groups (*Tony Eardley, 1989*).

Women's 'hidden' homelessness

In addition to the inadequate provision for homeless women, many women have, or feel that they have, obligations to husbands and children and, therefore, have little option but to stay in unsatisfactory or unsafe housing conditions. The fact that a woman may be partially or wholly financially dependent on a husband or partner further restricts her ability to escape from intolerable housing conditions.

The lack of provision for homeless women and the inadequate statistics and research leads to a tendency to see homelessness as a male problem. However, the Housing Advice Switchboard (HAS) based in London received 10,000 calls in 1988 about housing problems. Sixty per cent of these calls were from women (*HAS, 1989*).

The 1981 census showed that 30% of hostel and common lodging residents were women. In London researchers found that 36% of people staying in hostel and housing projects were women. Most notably, women made up half of all those under 26, indicating the size of the problem among young women (*Tony Eardley, 1988*).

In mixed accommodation, women are vulnerable to sexual harassment and abuse so for many women this is not an option they would freely choose. Nevertheless, the research shows that many women have to stay in mixed-sex temporary accommodation because they have nowhere else to go.

Hidden homelessness is a particular problem for many disabled women, such as women who are unable to leave hospitals or long-stay institutions or who are forced to remain in unsuitable dwellings and conditions.

Often temporary accommodation, including refuges for women escaping violence and emergency direct-access accommodation, are not accessible to disabled women, so there is literally nowhere for homeless disabled women to go.

More women in temporary accommodation

Growing homelessness has meant that more households are living in temporary accommodation because there is nowhere else for them to go. Returns from local authorities show that in 1984 nearly 11,000 households were living in bed and breakfast hotels and other forms of temporary accommodation in England and Wales. By the end of 1987, this had more than doubled to over 25,000 households. At the end of 1989, the figure was 37,900

Joanne O'Brien/FORMAT

Women occupying Camden Town Hall in 1984 in protest against the deaths of 3 Bengali people killed in a fire in a B & B hotel.

53

households in England alone (*Department of the Environment, 1989*).

Living in temporary accommodation is often the only housing option for women because of a lack of income and other resources. Research by Pat Niner and Andrew Thomas (1989) showed that 48% of households in temporary accommodation surveyed (1000 in total) contained no adult male. Forty per cent of all households surveyed were single parents. Unfortunately, as the housing crisis continues, bed and breakfast will remain a poor option but the only one for many homeless women.

Single women's homelessness

Because single women (and men) are not considered to be 'priority need' by local authorities and are not classified as 'homeless', there are no official estimates of single people's homelessness. However, CHAR, the housing campaign for single people, estimates that there are about two million single homeless people in Britain. The London Housing Unit estimate that there are about 64,500 single homeless persons in London alone (*Joe Oldman, 1989*).

At a recent seminar organised by the Scottish Council for Single Homeless (SCSH), researcher Sarah Webb spoke about her attempts to uncover women's hidden homelessness. She analysed Glasgow City Council's housing waiting list and found that 23,000 people were staying 'care of' another address. This figure accounted for 62% of the entire council waiting list. Five thousand of these were single women.

A representative of Clydebank local authority talked about research which revealed that 909 single men and 676 single women were registered on waiting lists using a 'care of' address. Women therefore formed 43% of single people without an address of their own. Researchers at the seminar concluded that there is a need for more monitoring by sex by local authorities so that the problem of women's homelessness can begin to be addressed (*SCSH, 1989*).

When relationships break down...

Women who have relied, at least partially, on a male partner for financial and other security are particularly vulnerable to homelessness when the relationship breaks down. Without savings and with poor employment prospects if they have been out of the labour market for long periods, women leaving relationships will have difficulty securing accommodation.

Returns from local authorities show that relationship breakdown is a major reason for homelessness: 17% of households were accepted by local authorities as homeless due to relationship breakdown in the last quarter of 1989 (*Department of Environment, 1989*).

Single parents: more likely to be homeless

Research by the London Housing Unit shows that a third of households in London accepted as homeless were single parents, and that single parents were more than eight times more likely to become homeless as other households. Nearly one-third of the single parents cited relationship break-down as their immediate reason for homelessness (*Danny Friedman and Hal Pawson, 1989*).

Escaping violence

A survey conducted by Women Against Rape in 1985 found that nearly three-quarters of the women interviewed who had tried to leave rapist husbands said that their biggest problem was that there was nowhere to live that they could afford.

Under current legislation, women escaping violence have no statutory right to accommodation. Local authorities are urged in the Code of Guidance to the legislation to 'secure wherever possible' accommodation for women fleeing violence with children. However, women without children who leave home because of domestic violence are not usually accepted as a priority group within the terms of Part III of the 1985 Housing Act.

Inevitably, local authorities vary in the degree of sympathy accorded to women and the action they take (or do not take). So, for example, many authorities do not accept single women fleeing violence as a priority category. Also, women are not generally considered to be a priority category if the abuse or threat of abuse comes from outside the household.

The Women's Aid Federation England (WAFE) say that the current housing crisis creates a bottleneck situation in refuges in which women are stuck for longer and longer periods because they are unable to find suitable permanent housing. This means that there may be no room in refuges for women fleeing violence. WAFE also say that many women who stay in refuges are forced to return to violent partners because there is nowhere else for them to go.

Young women – increasing homelessness

Homeless young women (and men) have no statutory right to accommodation (see chapter four). Research by Centrepoint suggests that in Central London alone at least 50,000 people under the age of 19 are homeless each year. Of these, about 2,000 are squatting in derelict buildings, 2,000 are in bed and breakfast hostels, 10,000 are living in hostels and 45,000 are staying temporarily with friends and relatives (*Alex Cosgrave, 1988*).

Many young women are forced to leave home before they want to (see chapter three). Young women in children's homes and young women leaving prison and detention centres are particularly likely to become homeless if they have no friends or relatives who will take them in (*Juliet Gosling, 1989*).

A teenage project in London, run by the Children's Society, housed 532 young runaways in their 'safe house' between 1987 and 1989. Fifty-three per cent of the runaway children were young women.

When the problem of young women's homelessness is addressed, specific issues are raised. One of these issues is sexual abuse. Statistics suggest that young women, more than young men, are vulnerable to sexual abuse both at home and outside the home (although this is not to deny that young men are also vulnerable to such abuse). Twenty-nine per cent of young women at the teenage project (and six per cent of young men) had been sexually abused in the past. Four per cent of young women gave sexual abuse at home as their immediate reason for running away (and no young men gave this as their reason).

One young woman at the project had been sexually abused by both her father and brother. Her mother found out and requested that the girl tell no one. She ran away out of desperation because she had no one to turn to (*Cathy Newman, 1989*).

The National Association of Young People In Care (NAYPIC), based in London, say that emotional, physical and sexual abuse is a regular occurrence for children in care. A pilot study conducted recently by NAYPIC showed there is a wide range of abuse in local authority homes and foster homes as well as in private homes. Over 30 different types of abuses were identified by NAYPIC, including neglect, the use of sedation and verbal abuse (*NAYPIC 1990*).

Young women who wish to escape from abuse by a trusted adult have particular needs in terms of both support and accommodation. Many young women today must be forced to remain with their abusers because there are no suitable housing and support networks.

Lesbians: invisible homelessness

There is still no official recognition of the vulnerability of lesbians and gays to homelessness and still little research and writing on the needs of homeless lesbians and gays. Yet people working in the field of housing suggest that homelessness is an increasing problem for lesbians and gays. For example, CHAR, the campaign for single homeless people say that increasingly lesbians (and gay men) are made homeless when they 'come out' to friends, parents and other relatives (*CHAR, 1988*).

The Central London Teenage Project found several young people had run away from home due to conflict over their sexuality. One young lesbian runaway at the project said her parents wanted her to choose friends from their local church and that, according to their religion, her lesbianism was a 'cardinal sin'.

Another 16 year old girl absconded from a children's home because staff at the home frowned on her lesbian relationship with another girl and had restricted her movements (*Cathy Newman, 1989*).

The problem of homelessness among lesbians is one which demands further research and attention from researchers, housing providers and policy makers alike.

Conclusion

Probably the most direct cause of women's homelessness is a lack of affordable and decent housing in both the public and private sectors. Women's low income places them at a disadvantage in securing suitable housing. Housing providers and policy makers must begin to take women's specific housing needs and problems seriously, so that their homelessness is no longer an invisible problem ■

chapter five

WOMEN AND NATIONAL HOUSING POLICY

Jackie is a single parent receiving income support and living in privately rented accommodation. Her rent is £25 a week. However, the local authority rent office set her rent at £16 a week and this is all that her housing benefit will cover. She, therefore, has to find £9 a week out of her income support.

This has inevitably led to rent arrears. Coupled with these problems, Jackie is being harassed by her landlord, who enters the property unannounced at any time and rings her in the middle of the night demanding the rent.

This chapter explores the effects of national housing policy over the past decade on women's access to housing and shows, particularly, how women are increasingly losing out because of a system based on ability to pay, rather than on need.

National housing policy

Housing policy, similarly to other social policies, has traditionally been, and continues to be, based on assumptions about the 'family' and women's role within families (see chapter two). Such assumptions disadvantage women within conventional families as they do not have equal access to income, housing and other resources. It also disadvantages other household types, such as single people, single parents and lesbian and gay couples.

Three broad objectives emerged in national housing policy during the 1980s: to increase home-ownership; to revitalise the private rented sector; and to reduce the role of local authorities in providing and managing housing.

Despite incentives in the form of tax relief on mortgage interest, home-ownership remains beyond the means of women on low incomes. Current housing policy represents a move towards a housing system which is based on ability to pay, rather than need. Women are disproportionately disadvantaged by this because of their low incomes and the fact that more women than men rely on councils for accommodation.

Deregulating private rented housing

Since the introduction of the 1988 Housing Act, tenants have less security of tenure and pay higher rents. The Act introduced 'assured' and 'assured shorthold' tenancies. A tenant who accepts a shorthold tenancy has no security of tenure and can be evicted at the end of a fixed term (*Les Burrows, 1989*).

Under the Act, the new registration of 'fair rents' was abolished. Instead 'market' rents can be charged i.e. landlords have the freedom to set rents at whatever price they think they can get.

Rent officers, while keeping some of their old 'fair rent' role for pre-1988 tenancies, assess new tenancies on whether rents are 'reasonable' for the purpose of subsidy on the basis of 'market rents' within the area. If a rent is considered higher than the average market rent, housing benefit officers will restrict rent payments.

Rising rents, together with cuts in housing benefit inevitably hit low-income households, and particularly women, hardest. At the same time, reduced security of tenure means women are more vulnerable to harassment by landlords. Research shows that increasing numbers of landlords are trying to get tenants out of their homes following the passing of the 1988 Housing Act. Black and ethnic minority women, lesbians and older women are among those most vulnerable to harassment (see *Les Burrows and Neil Hunter, 1990*).

No rights of succession: carers losing out

The 1988 Housing Act also drastically reduced people's rights of succession. Spouses (including recognised partners) retain rights of succession but women who care for older or disabled relatives at home are particularly hard hit. Under the terms of the Act, relatives will only have the right to succeed to a Rent Act statutory tenancy if they have lived in the property for more than two years. Previously it was only six months. Many women who have moved in with older or disabled relatives who had assured tenancies for less than two years will have no rights of succession and may face homelessness. Relatives of assured tenants (virtually all tenancies since January 1989) have no right of succession at all, no matter what the circumstances.

Given the changes in legislation which both increase rents and reduce security of tenure for tenants, it is increasingly likely that women's housing needs will not be adequately met in the private rented sector.

Undermining the role of housing associations

The Government is currently abdicating responsibility for housing provision and looking towards housing associations to provide more accommodation for households who cannot afford, or do not wish, to buy their homes. As was pointed out in chapter two, housing associations have traditionally provided homes for low-income families, households whose needs are not met in the public sector, such as single people, and people who face discrimination by landlords on grounds such as age, race, sex and sexuality.

This role is in danger of being undermined. In the current housing crisis, housing associations are under pressure both to charge higher rents and to provide housing for more conventional household types.

The 1988 Housing Act introduced mixed funding for housing associations who now receive only an average of 85% of their grant from central government. Before 1988, any deficit would be made up by central government in the way of deficit funding. Now, housing associations are dependent on the rents received from tenants to bridge the gap between private and government subsidies – and rents are rising to cover the costs.

Housing associations are now moving up-market: private finance is more readily available to fund new build developments outside inner-city areas. Because their growth is dependent on the use of private finance, there are now fears that housing associations are catering more for people who can afford to pay, rather than those most in need. Women on low incomes will inevitably now lose out.

Decreasing council housing: reducing women's choices

More women than men rely on council housing, particularly divorced and separated women and single parents. The last decade has seen a drastic reduction in the council houses available for rent, reducing women's chances of being allocated a property and of transferring from an unsuitable property in this sector.

A major consequence of Government policy on public expenditure on housing has been a rapid fall in new construction. The number of new council houses built in England has fallen from 79,009 in 1979 to just 14,925 in 1989 (*Housing and Construction Statistics, 1974-84 September 1989*).

Simultaneously, the number of households requiring council accommodation has actually increased: In 1983 there were 741,000 households on waiting lists in England. By 1988 this figure had risen to 1,268,000 (*Joe Oldman, 1989*).

The right-to-buy legislation introduced in 1980 has led to the sale of over 1.1 million council houses in England and Wales (*Hansard, 24.1.90*).

Research conducted by the London Research Centre (1989) showed that households buying their homes under the right-to-buy legislation in London were overwhelmingly couples and couples with children (88% in total). People not taking advantage of the legislation include single people (only one per cent of buyers), pensioners (10% of buyers) and single parents (just two per cent of buyers). Because of the higher proportions of women in all these categories, it seems likely that more women are not taking advantage of the right-to-buy legislation.

The trend towards reducing the role of local authorities in the provision and management of housing culminated in the 1980s with the wholesale transfer of estates to private developers. Under the 1988 Housing Act estates can be sold off to private landlords unless a majority of tenants voted against it (with abstentions counting as votes in favour of privatisation).

At the moment, it is London authorities who are leading the way in the privatisation of estates, for example, Wandsworth, Westminster and Kensington and Chelsea. However, many local authorities outside London are currently considering estate disposal as the solution to the problem of decaying

Is the sale of council estates the solution to the problem of decaying stock and low public investment? Many housing authorities think so but many tenants disagree.

stock and reduced public investment, irrespective of political orientation (and some large-scale voluntary transfers have taken place).

A survey by the London Housing Unit showed that there are important differences between previous tenants and new residents on some of the privatised estates in London. Most of the new residents in estates such as the Falcons in Wandsworth, the Waterlow in Tower Hamlets and the Elgin in Westminster are overwhelmingly young professionals or white-collar workers without children. Sixty-six per cent were under 30, 84% were white and most households had incomes averaging £20,000 a year (*London Housing News, April 1988*).

The council tenants who were moved out to make way for such schemes were all found to have incomes of below £5,000 a year. Many were on state benefits, just 37% were in full-time work, 29% were retired and 23% were aged 65 or over, with only 13% of tenants under the age of 30 (*London Housing News, April 1988*).

In many areas, such as London's Docklands, urban development grants have enabled authorities to revitalise whole areas. However, there is evidence that such schemes are being entered into without due concern for the needs of low-income families in the area. In the Docklands area, 83% of housing was owned by local councils prior to the developments in the early 1980s. For example, new build by private developers was primarily for owner-occupation which was beyond the means of most local people. High value developments such as office blocks and luxury flats have replaced previous rented housing and community facilities in the Docklands and there is concern that existing housing and other facilities are not meeting the needs of low-income people, many of which will be women (*Joint Docklands Action Group, 1987*).

Because women generally have lower incomes than men, it is likely that they will figure strongly among the people losing out as more councils seek privatisation as the answer to housing problems. In the face of dramatic cuts in public expenditure, combined with increasing sales, women's opportunities for accommodation in the council sector have narrowed.

Conclusion

The overall effects of housing policy in the last decade have been to tie access to housing more closely to income rather than need. Because of their low incomes, women are disproportionately losing out and face increasing difficulties in getting affordable, decent housing. The inevitable result of current trends is rising homelessness. Women will increasingly find themselves facing homelessness due to a lack of suitable and affordable housing options.

In such a climate it is essential that housing providers and policy makers begin to take the issue of women's housing needs and experiences seriously ■

PART II

A study of women's access to housing on the Trinity Estate, Salford.

chapter six

INTRODUCTION

The purpose of the case study was to gain further information about women's access to housing and the effects of national housing policy, focusing particularly on the issue of the privatisation of council housing. This study is the first of its kind.

Salford was chosen as the case study area because it provides an example of an area where the local authority has enthusiastically embarked on the wholesale privatisation of council housing. Also, it was thought to be an interesting area for study because Salford City is a Labour-controlled council which is following the Conservative government's policy of reducing the public provision of housing and simultaneously promoting owner-occupation. We wanted to find out if women were losing out because of privatisation policies in Salford.

Within Salford, the Trinity estate was chosen for detailed analysis because it provides an example of an estate where substantial numbers of properties have been sold off to private developers and then re-sold on the open market. We wanted to see what access women have to housing on the Trinity estate.

Privatisation in Salford

Throughout the 1950s and 1960s the main thrust of Salford City's housing policy was slum clearance and new build. In the 1970s and early 1980s the council concentrated on directing limited and declining resources into the maintenance of existing housing stock.

By the early 1980s public housing comprised the largest sector of housing in Salford: 47% of households lived in council accommodation in 1981. However, despite the dominance of the council sector, Salford City did not appear to have an overall housing policy. Housing officers characterised the authority's policy prior to 1984 as 'ad-hoc' and 'reactive' (*Michael Bradford and Andrew Steward, 1988*).

In 1983, a working party on housing policy was set up by Salford City Council which noted three major housing problems in Salford. These were:-

- The poor condition of local authority stock and particularly the 49% comprised of flats and maisonettes. Estates suffered from low occupancy levels, high voids, vandalism and high numbers of repairs outstanding.

- The mismatch between type of stock and demand in the local authority sector, and in particular, a demand for 'family housing' as opposed to single person flatted accommodation which dominated the council stock.

- There was a low level of owner-occupation, particularly in the inner areas (just 42% of households owned their homes in 1981, compared to 47% living in council accommodation). This was seen as contributing to the declining population in Salford (the population had fallen from 279,000 in 1971 to 241,522 in 1981) since it meant people were buying outside the area because of a lack of properties for sale within Salford itself (*Michael Bradford and Andrew Steward, 1988*).

An additional problem was that Salford City was facing severe cuts in housing expenditure. Between 1979 and 1983 the allocation for expenditure on housing under the Housing Investment Programme (HIP) was reduced from £35,000,000 to £28,387,000. The Council saw that the reduction in resources was likely to continue (and indeed, by 1989/90 the allocation was just £8,170,000 – in real terms, a tenth of the 1979 figure).

In an attempt to deal with the housing problems, the Council embarked on a 'partnership' with the private sector. By selling off substantial parts of estates to private developers, and with the aid of a grant from central government (over half of which was dependent upon private sector involvement), Salford City were able to refurbish some of the remaining council stock without substantial expenditure.

In April 1983 the Ordsall flats, close to the city centre and comprising 208 dwellings, were sold to Barratt Urban Renewal with vacant possession. The estate had a history of high void rates, high turnover of tenants, and a poor record on repairs.

The Council had considered demolishing the blocks in the early 1980s. Instead, the flats were turned over to Barratts, at a total price of £50,000. Thirty-eight flats were demolished by Barratts and the remaining 170 were completely modernised and refurbished. The estate was renamed 'Regents Park' and the properties were then sold on the open market at prices of between £16,000 and £20,000 each.

The same year, Salford City sold 114 empty maisonettes in St. Stephen Street, adjacent to the Trinity estate, to property developers Barratts for a total price of £100,000. Barratts demolished 15 flats, refurbished the remaining 99 properties and sold them a year later on the open market at prices of between £15,500 and £19,250.

Similar initiatives followed at Canterbury Gardens (formally the Ladywell flats), St James' Park (the Langwell flats) and Crescent Court.

Salford City Council had three main aims in embarking on the partnership with the private sector in Salford:-

■ To shed unneeded flats in the City and replace them with 'family' accommodation, by which the council meant conventional heterosexual, two-parent families.

■ To widen people's housing choices in Salford, by introducing a mix of flats and houses, council accommodation and privately owned housing.

■ To improve the environment and image of the inner-city.

From the point of view of Salford City Council the aims of the public/private partnership have been met. The partnership is part of a successful promotional strategy, presenting a glossy new image for Salford and showing what can be achieved in run-down areas. The local authority uses the developments as symbols to attract both central government finance and private investment to Salford.

However, many local people and groups are openly critical of privatisation in Salford. Keith Argyle, of Salford Urban Mission, was an active campaigner against the initiative. His research suggests that local people were unable to benefit from the newly available housing stock because of its high price – only five per cent of the original inhabitants in St. Stephen Street were in a position to afford the terms of the mortgages. Keith Argyle concluded that privatisation does not meet the needs of low-income families in Salford (*Keith Argyle, 1988*).

Researchers Michael Bradford and Andrew Steward found that most of the council tenants on the Trinity estate adjacent to St. Stephen Street felt the scheme to be divisive as it showed them the kinds of homes which they knew they could not afford. Some tenants even felt that the improvements in St. Stephen Street had accelerated the decline of the rest of Trinity (*Michael Bradford and Andrew Steward, 1988*).

The Trinity estate

The Trinity estate lies within half a mile of Manchester's commercial centre. Built early in the 1960s, it comprised a mixture of deck-access maisonettes, three-storey flats and high-rise blocks. The estate originally held 1001 dwellings and, in its day, was a show-piece. However, documents from Salford City Council show that by 1983 it was visibly run-down, with high levels of under-occupation (46%) and voids (20%) (*City Council Social Survey, 1985*).

View of Trinity estate from a high-rise block.

The council's solution to the problem was to enter into a partnership with Barratts, selling off approximately two-thirds of the estate and retaining one-third as council accommodation. The outcome of the partnership was that Salford City kept possession of the deck-access maisonettes, decapitating them and transforming them into terraced and semi-detached houses with gardens. Twenty new bungalows were built by the council for rent to older people. Several blocks of high-rise flats were 'landscaped', and security at the flats was improved. This was funded with the help of government grants (44% of the project budget). Over half of the government money (an urban programme grant) was dependent on private involvement.

Barratts were sold the least popular high-rise stock which was demolished and replaced with low-rise flats and houses. They were put up for sale on the open market at prices of between £42,000 and £52,000.

A large number of the tenants were moved out by the council during refurbishment and were informed that whoever wanted to come back to the estate on completion of the project would be able to. Salford City could apparently make this assertion with a fair degree of confidence since their own survey had shown that many people on Trinity (47%) preferred to be rehoused elsewhere. However, research suggests that many people who wanted to come back to the estate were not able to (see, for example, *Jon May, 1989*). Also, our questionnaire survey suggests that the council tenants who are now on the estate are mostly those who simply refused to move ■

chapter seven

THE QUESTIONNAIRE SURVEY

During January and February 1990, a questionnaire survey was conducted, door-to-door, on the Trinity estate to examine the effect of privatisation on access to housing for different types of households on the estate. Two-hundred and twenty-four households agreed to be interviewed. The results of the survey are outlined below. Details of the research methodology are given in the appendix, page 98.

We wanted to analyse the responses of women and men on the estate by age and marital status. However, this was found to be unsatisfactory because of the small sample size, particularly where only a small number of respondents had answered a question and where a diverse range of answers were given by respondents.

We have, therefore, used the conventional terms 'female-headed' and 'male-headed' households, although it is recognised that these terms are not wholly satisfactory because they imply the dominance of men within households.

The analysis showed that the differences in responses between female and male-headed households, when defined in this way, were negligible (apart from 'preferences for renting or buying' – see page 80). By far the greatest differences were between council tenants and home-owners. However, the survey showed clearly that women form the majority of council tenants on the estate (as they do nationally). Conversely, men form the majority of home-owners (as nationally). The results below confirm the value of looking at the differences between council tenants and home-owners in order to examine women's access to housing on the Trinity estate.

Composition of the estate

As the diagram on p.69 shows, council housing on Trinity is in the process of being rapidly reduced, from 99% of total housing on the estate in 1980, to just 60% of the total housing in 1990. By 1991/2, when the project is due to be finished, the council sector will comprise just 29% of the total housing on the estate. This picture of decreasing council housing on the Trinity estate mirrors the national picture of council housing over the past decade as more and more is sold off under the right-to-buy legislation and to private developers (see chapter five).

Figure 3
Actual and proposed housing in Trinity and St. Stephens Street

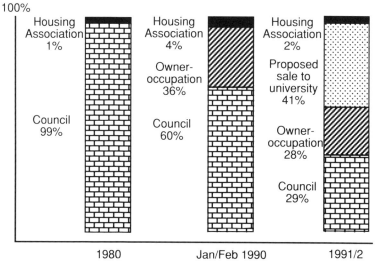

Note: Of the 41% to be sold to the university it is proposed that about 27% will be rented to students and 14% to a housing association.

Sources: City of Salford Trinity Project Area Profile. Ref. TR1 AAA, Trinity Area Project office and observation by research team at the time of the Shelter survey.

At the time of the Shelter survey in January and February 1990, building on the estate was still in progress. As of April 1990, the future of 41% of the housing stock on Trinity (three blocks of unoccupied high-rise flats) was still uncertain. However, it is proposed that the blocks be sold to a local housing association. It is thought that two of the three blocks will be sub-let to a local University for rent specifically to students.

The owner-occupied sector on the Trinity estate consists of one-three bedroomed flats and two-three bedroomed houses, all newly built. Several of the flats appeared to be unoccupied at the time of the survey. One respondent told us that the flat above her had been bought by a businessman as an 'investment', and had remained unoccupied since it was sold. Almost all of the privately owned houses appeared to be occupied at the time of the survey, although several houses had 'for sale' notices in the gardens and we were unable to contact the occupiers.

The council sector now comprises three main types of property. These are, firstly, two-three bedroomed houses, which were refurbished internally and externally. The houses are comparatively popular and were all occupied at the time of the survey.

Secondly, the estate contains high-rise flats – seven storeys – which had not had any internal refurbishment and had only had limited external improvements. The high-rise flats were unpopular with many tenants and the blocks contained many boarded and unoccupied properties, particularly on the higher storeys.

Finally, the estate contains a block of low-rise flats (refurbished) and a block of newly-built bungalows which are specifically for rent to pensioner households. These are popular among older people on the estate and many older people living in the high-rise flats expressed a wish to live in the pensioner properties. All of the pensioner properties were occupied at the time of the survey.

At the time of the survey, a six-foot fence was in the process of being erected in the middle of the estate, effectively fencing-in the home-owners and simultaneously fencing-out the council tenants.

Some council tenants we spoke to now have to walk round the estate to get to the local shops that are at the end of their gardens and were understandably unhappy about the situation. In effect, the fence symbolises the split of the estate into two main tenures. Many local people in Salford feel that this creates ghettos and perhaps in the future, there will effectively be two Trinity Estates – one private and one council.

Household type by age and marital status

The diagram on p.72 shows that the largest group of home-owners on the Trinity estate (27%) are married or cohabiting couples without children. Households with two or more adults and men living alone also comprise comparatively large proportions of home-owners on the estate (each comprising 21% of total home-owners).

Interestingly, of the home-owning households with two or more adults, only three per cent were all-female households, while 37% were all-male households (the remaining 60% were mixed adult households).

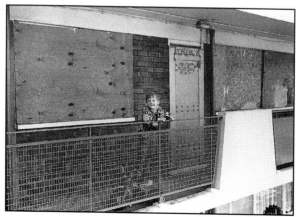

One estate, a range of tenures. Trinity estate, anti-clockwise, from top: showhouse for owner-occupied properties; newly built council bungalows for pensioners; boarded-up flat in high-rise council block; refurbished council home.

Figure 4

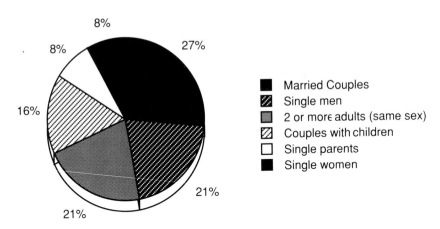

Owner-occupiers

- ■ Married Couples
- ▨ Single men
- ▦ 2 or more adults (same sex)
- ▧ Couples with children
- ☐ Single parents
- ■ Single women

Note: 63 home-owners agreed to take part in the survey and answered the question about household type.

Just 16% of home-owners (10) were married or cohabiting couples with children. Significantly, only eight per cent (five) of home-owners were single women and the same number were single parents. Ninety per cent of the single parents were women which is consistent with the national proportion.

The diagram also shows that there were no older men and women home-owners (that is, of pensionable age) on the Trinity estate. The absence of older home-owners is partially explained by the fact that the Barratts properties were aimed primarily at young, first-time buyers. It seems, therefore, that older people, the majority of whom are women due to their greater longevity, do not have access to home-ownership on the Trinity estate.

It is clear from the figures about household types on the Trinity estate that more men than women have access to home-ownership on the Trinity estate, similar to the situation in Britain generally, shown in Part I of the report. At the same time, the way women can best improve their chances of becoming home-owners on the Trinity estate, as in Britain generally, is in partnership with a man.

The diagram on p.73 shows that older women (that is, of pensionable age) living alone comprise the largest group among council tenants (24% or 33 women). Older men comprise 10% (14) of council tenants and older couples, 12% (16). Overall, 46% of households in the council sector are pensioner households. The high number of pensioner households is explained in part by the type of housing, a large proportion of which is for rent specifically to older people.

Figure 5

Council tenants

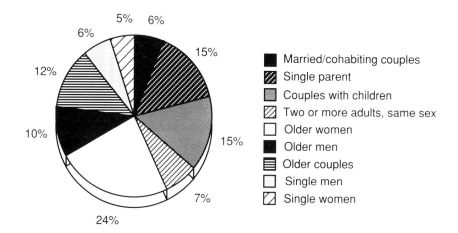

5% 6%
6%
15%
12%
10%
15%
7%
24%

■ Married/cohabiting couples
▨ Single parent
▦ Couples with children
▧ Two or more adults, same sex
☐ Older women
■ Older men
≡ Older couples
☐ Single men
▨ Single women

Note: 141 council tenants agreed to take part in the survey, 137 answered the question about household type.

Most of the older women council tenants living alone were located in the pensioner properties. However, it is significant that 33% of older women on Trinity were living in the high-rise flats, in relatively poor housing conditions and unsuitable properties. Fifty per cent of older couples and fifty per cent of older men also lived in the high-rise flats.

The diagram above also shows that 15% (21) of council tenants were single parents, almost all of whom were women. Most of the single parents lived in the refurbished council properties and had obtained access to these because they had always lived on the estate. However, they felt that they were there because they had refused to be moved when the estate was refurbished and that if they had moved they would not have been able to come back.

The diagram also shows that only five per cent of council tenants on the Trinity estate are single women (and six per cent are single men). This illustrates the point that on the Trinity estate, similar to the national position, single women (and also single men) do not generally have access to council accommodation.

The evidence from the analysis of the estate composition by household type shows that, overall, there were over twice as many women-only households who were council tenants as men-only households (43% compared to 20%). Conversely, there were nearly three times as many men-only households who were home-owners than women (40% compared to 16%) So, women rely to a larger extent than men on the council sector and fewer women than men have access to home-ownership, as in Britain generally (see Part I of the report).

Socio-economic groups on the Trinity estate

Figure 6

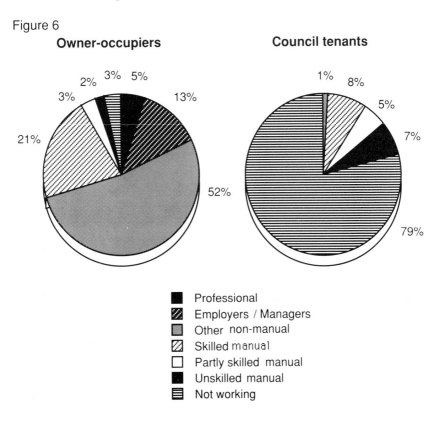

| Owner-occupiers | Council tenants |

■ Professional
▨ Employers / Managers
☐ Other non-manual
▨ Skilled manual
☐ Partly skilled manual
■ Unskilled manual
☰ Not working

Note: Two people did not respond to the question about socio-economic status.

The diagram shows that home-owners on the Trinity estate are overwhelmingly located in higher socio-economic groups than council tenants. This supports the generally accepted view, that the council sector is occupied by those on low incomes.

Among council tenants, 79% were out of work. Of the employed respondents, most were skilled manual workers. At the same time, all of the home-owners, bar two, were working. Fifty-one (85%) of these were in full-time work and seven (12%) were in part-time work. Most respondents (52%) were other non-manual workers.

Disabled people on the Trinity estate

Forty-one (19%) of the 212 people responding to the question about disability said that they were either registered as disabled or considered themselves to be disabled.

A further 10 people (five per cent) said that there was someone else in the house who was registered as, or considered themselves to be, disabled.

Most disabled respondents were women (53% compared to 47% who were men), which is consistent with the national picture of disabled people. Although two-thirds of the disabled respondents were over pension age (again, reflecting the national picture), one-third of the respondents were of working age and 14% were under the age of 40.

The most common types of disability mentioned by respondents were heart attack or stroke (nine people), difficulty in walking (seven people), arthritis (seven people), impaired vision (seven people), and bronchitis (seven people).

Most of the disabled respondents were living on state benefits. Only four (eight per cent) were in full-time work. This is consistent with the picture nationally, as outlined in Part I of the report – disabled people generally have less access to employment and income than non-disabled people and are, therefore, generally poorer than non-disabled people.

Thirty-one per cent of the disabled respondents lived in the high-rise flats – properties which are totally unsuitable for many disabled people. Furthermore, a majority of those in the high-rise flats lived on the fourth floor or above.

'I wish I could have a lift put in' says Jane, aged 92. She is unable to climb her stairs without help.

Adaptations for disabled people

The overwhelming majority of respondents (95%) said that their homes were not adapted at all for people with disabilities. Only four per cent (nine) said there were some kind of adaptations. These adaptations were minor, such as handles on baths.

Of the respondents who were registered as disabled or considered themselves to be disabled, 86% said that their homes were not adapted at all for people with disabilities. Interestingly, 74% of the disabled respondents said that their homes did not need any adaptations. Many of these respondents were older people (and most were older women) who seemed to accept their situation and did not expect any help from anyone. One respondent, an older woman, lived on the fifth floor of the high-rise flats and was unable to use the stairs because she had difficulty walking. She did not feel that she needed any adaptations because *we're all like this at my age'*.

This acceptance of unsatisfactory housing conditions provides a striking illustration of the powerlessness experienced by disabled people.

Ethnic origin

The overwhelming majority (90%) of tenants on the estate who responded to the question about ethnic origin (213 people) described themselves as 'White UK'.

All of the respondents in the council sector were white European. This raises the question of the access that black and ethnic minority groups have to the Trinity estate. Unfortunately, there was not scope within the Trinity survey to investigate this aspect further. However, the question of the particular needs and experiences of black and ethnic minority women in Salford is dealt with in some detail in chapter eight.

Figure 7

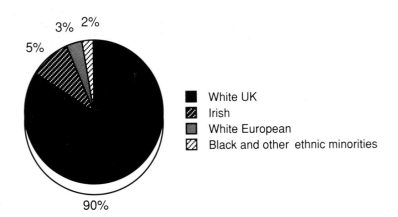

■ White UK
▨ Irish
▦ White European
▨ Black and other ethnic minorities

As it was pointed out in the first part of the report, very few local authorities carry out ethnic monitoring so the discrimination black and ethnic minority people face in access to housing normally remains hidden from view.

Sexuality

Of those who answered the question about sexuality (195 people out of 224), six per cent (11) said that they were lesbian or gay. A further six respondents said that another person in the household was lesbian or gay. Most of the lesbian and gay respondents (82%) were home-owners. Just 18% (two) were council tenants.

As it was pointed out in the first part of this report, there is very little data on the housing needs and experiences of lesbians (and also of gay men) nationally and there is clearly a need for more research at both national and local levels. Unfortunately, there was not scope within the Trinity survey to do this. The housing experiences of one lesbian living in Salford are described below in ' women's voices '.

Satisfaction with accommodation

Figure 8

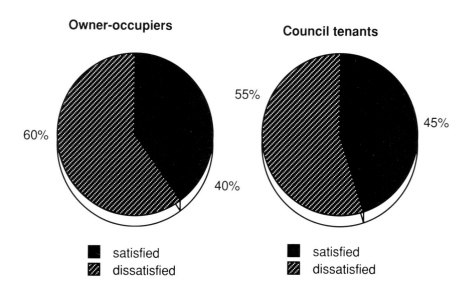

Owner-occupiers

55%

60%

40%

Council tenants

45%

■ satisfied
▨ dissatisfied

■ satisfied
▨ dissatisfied

Fifty-five per cent (112) of the respondents answering the question about satisfaction with accommodation said that they were dissatisfied in some way. Just 45% (90) were satisfied.

The diagram on p.77 shows that a larger proportion of home-owners (60%), most of whom are men, were dissatisfied in some way with their homes than council tenants (55%), most of whom are women.

Interestingly, the largest proportion of satisfied council tenants are living in the high-rise flats (61% were satisfied with their homes). At the same time, only 33% of the respondents living in the newly refurbished council houses were satisfied. Forty-five per cent of the people in the pensioner properties were satisfied with their homes. Women formed the majority of council tenants in all three types of council accommodation on the estate.

The comparatively high level of satisfaction among pensioners in the pensioner properties can be partially explained by the relatively high standard of the accommodation, and also by the fact that many pensioners had low expectations of their housing situation. The English House Condition Survey (1986) confirms that older people are generally more likely to be satisfied with their homes than younger people.

At first sight, it seems surprising that higher proportions of home-owners and council tenants in the newly refurbished council houses are dissatisfied. However, the large degree of dissatisfaction can be linked to the higher expectations of the home-owners and the council tenants in the newly refurbished properties. For many people, these expectations seem now to be largely unfulfilled (see discussion below).

Also, a high proportion of tenants in the high-rise council flats (42%) are older people (31% of whom are older women on their own) who would have low expectations about their housing situation. Although some tenants in the high-rise flats did complain bitterly about their homes, most residents were resigned to the fact that there were unlikely to be any improvements.

Reasons for dissatisfaction

Among both council tenants and home-owners, the major reason for dissatisfaction was the poor standard of the building. Both home-owners and council tenants complained about poor finishing and other structural defects and both said they had had difficulties in getting poor work remedied.

The second biggest complaint among council tenants was internal structure. Many of the complaints in the high-rise council flats were about things like badly-fitting and draughty windows.

In the refurbished council houses a common complaint was about the patio doors which looked attractive but were a source of annoyance as they were a cause of heat loss. Also, they were the only access to the back garden and were not practical for everyday use.

Many home-owners were dissatisfied with the area, complaining it was 'unsightly'. However, this complaint was not just restricted to home-owners as a large number of council tenants also complained about this.

The responses to this question show that it is the physical condition of housing that is important and not just the type of tenure. The results of our survey show clearly that owner-occupation is not a panacea for housing. This begs the question as to whether more investment in the condition of the existing housing would have produced a higher level of satisfaction than the creation of another type of tenure.

Desire to stay in present accommodation

We asked respondents whether they wished to stay in their current accommodation for the next two years. The results of the survey show that despite the number of people who were dissatisfied with aspects of their accommodation, the vast majority (88%) wanted to stay where they were for the next two years.

All of the people in the pensioner properties who answered the question about staying in their accommodation (most of whom were women) wanted to stay for the next two years. Almost all of the older people said they were too old to move again.

Ninety-six per cent of tenants in the refurbished council houses and 75% of the tenants in the high-rise council flats wanted to stay in their homes for the next two years. Most of these were women. Among home-owners, most of whom were men, a much lower proportion (78%) said they wished to stay for the next two years. It is likely that a lot of the home-owners saw their house as a step on the property ladder and did not have any real attachment to the estate. Significantly, a comparatively high proportion of home-owners (22%) saw home-ownership on the estate as just a short-term option. On the other hand, many tenants in the council properties did have an attachment to the estate and wanted to remain where they were.

Housing preferences

We asked respondents whether they would prefer to rent or buy, given the choice. A slightly higher proportion of male-headed households than female-headed said that they would prefer to buy (46% compared to 32%). Conversely, a slightly higher proportion of female-headed households said that they would prefer to rent.

These differences can be explained by the fact that male-headed households generally have higher incomes than female-headed households. Home-buying is, therefore, a more realistic option for male-headed households than female-headed households. However, by far the biggest differences in preferences were between council tenants (most of whom are women) and owner-occupiers (most of whom are men). These differences are shown in the diagram below.

Preferences for renting or buying

Figure 9

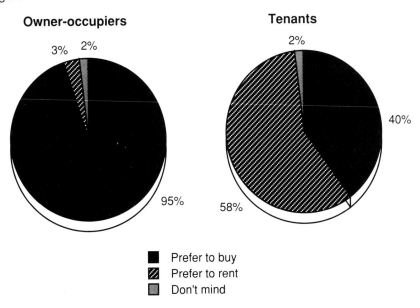

Owner-occupiers   Tenants

■ Prefer to buy
▨ Prefer to rent
▩ Don't mind

Note: 217 out of 224 responded to the question about preferences for renting or buying.

As the diagram above shows, almost all home-owners (95% or 59 people) said that, given the choice, they would prefer to buy their homes. Only three per cent (two) said they would prefer to rent. Conversely, most council tenants said that they would prefer to rent their homes (58% or 79 people). Only 40% (54) said they would prefer to buy.

The differences in quality and desirability of the council tenures on the estate are reflected in the differing proportions of tenants who said they would prefer to buy their homes. In the refurbished council houses, 77% said that they would prefer to buy, while only 23% preferred to rent. Conversely, in the high-rise flats, 80% said they would prefer to rent and only 20% said they would prefer to buy.

In the pensioner properties, 87% preferred to rent, and only 13% to buy, reflecting the fact that older residents had rented for most of their lives and felt they were too old to buy now. Many of the older people we spoke to said that they would consider buying if they were younger.

80

Preferences among council tenants

The major reasons for preferring to rent among council tenants was *'lack of money'* (48%), followed by *'too old to buy'* (34%). Interestingly, only five people gave 'positive' reasons for renting (for example, *'security'* and *'renting is easier'*). This suggests that renting is the most realistic option for low-income council tenants who are mostly women.

Most council tenants who said they would prefer to buy gave the reason that they would have their own home (38%). The next biggest reason (24%) was financial gain, including *'home-owning is an investment'*, *'it's cheaper in the long run'* and *'renting is a waste of money'*.

Almost all (95%) of the home-owners on the Trinity estate said that they preferred to buy. The biggest reason given for buying was financial gain (46%). *'independence'* (18%) and *'security'* (11%) were also popular reasons given by home-owners for preferring to buy.

Council tenants' ability to buy

Although home-ownership was seen as desirable by a large number of council tenants, only 24% (17) thought that they would be able to buy their homes within the next two years. A large majority (69%) said that they would not be able to buy their homes with seven per cent saying they did not know whether they would be able to or not.

There was no significant difference between the responses of female-headed and male-headed households to this question. However, because most council tenants on the estate are women and because council tenants generally have low incomes, it is women, rather than men, whose ability to buy is curtailed.

Applications to buy homes

Only 11% (15) of council tenants who wanted to buy their own homes had actually applied to the council to buy. Of these over half (nine) were couples with children. No single parents and no single women had applied to buy their homes.

This suggests that, however attractively and convincingly home-ownership is presented, it is something which people on low-incomes, and particularly women, cannot actually achieve.

It is clear that a large number of council tenants on the Trinity estate do not see home-ownership as a real choice given their economic circumstances. As it was pointed out earlier, more women than men on the estate are council tenants. It is clear therefore that women, more than men, do not see home-ownership as a real choice and are losing out from the increasing numbers of homes for sale on the Trinity estate.

Access to the Trinity estate

Figure 10

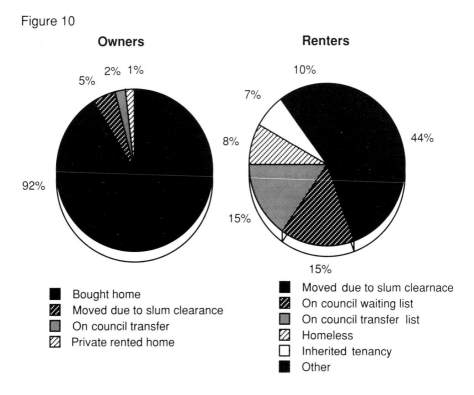

Owners	Renters
■ Bought home	■ Moved due to slum clearnace
▨ Moved due to slum clearance	▨ On council waiting list
▢ On council transfer	▢ On council transfer list
▨ Private rented home	▨ Homeless
	▢ Inherited tenancy
	■ Other

We asked respondents how they originally got access to the Trinity estate (not necessarily the property they now lived in).

The diagram above shows that home-owners (mostly men) overwhelmingly got access to the estate through buying their homes (92% of home-owners) and were, therefore, relative newcomers to the estate. Just eight per cent of home-owners had previously lived in rented property on the estate.

Conversely, most council tenants (mostly women) got access to the estate because they were '*in need*'. Forty-four per cent (66) of council tenants responding to the question were transferred from another property by the council due to slum clearance. These tenants were mostly women who had lived on the estate for long periods of their lives. A quarter of council tenants on the estate now are older women living alone.

As the proportion of council accommodation on the Trinity estate has gone down, less people get access to the estate because of need and access is now primarily gained through ability to buy. Women form the majority of council tenants who gained access to the estate because of need. At the same time, women form the minority of home-owners who are able to buy their way onto the estate. This raises the question of what happens to those in need now (most of whom will be women), who cannot buy their way into the housing market because of their low incomes.

These results support the argument outlined in Part I of the report that current housing policies mean access to housing is geared towards ability to pay, rather than need. Women are inevitably losing out.

Main conclusions from the questionnaire survey

■ The council wanted to widen people's housing choices in Salford by intro-ducing a mix of flats and houses, council and private accommodation. In reality, choices have not been widened for low-income families in Salford and particularly not for women. The survey showed that women have very little access to home-ownership. At the same time, opportunities in the council sector have actually narrowed because of the drastic cuts in available council accommodation.

■ Nine out of ten people on the Trinity estate described themselves as 'White UK'. Black and ethnic minority households, therefore, do not have access to the estate. It seems that housing choices for black and ethnic minority households in Salford have not been widened through the council's policy of privatisation.

■ Privatisation has been hailed as the 'way forward' in the 1990s in Salford, as in Britain generally. However, nearly two-thirds of home-owners on the estate (and over half of the council tenants) were dissatisfied with their homes. It seems that it is the physical condition of housing that is important to people, not just the type of tenure. This suggests that privatisation is not necessarily the answer to housing problems.

■ The survey showed that a large number of people on the estate were registered as disabled or considered themselves to be disabled but only a small percentage of properties were adapted in any way for disabled people. Many disabled tenants on the estate were found to be living in properties which were totally unsuitable for their needs.

■ Access to the estate is now primarily for those who can afford to buy a home. Most women on the estate only have access to home-ownership when they are living with a husband or male partner. Most council tenants (the majority of whom were women) said they would not be able to buy their homes. Pri-vatisation means people in need, and particularly women, are losing out■

chapter eight

THE WIDER CONTEXT

We wanted to put the questionnaire survey in a wider context, by looking at housing policy in Salford and the effects of this on women's access to housing. Due to time constraints, it was beyond the scope of this project to analyse in detail the housing needs of different groups of women. We therefore looked particularly at homeless women, black and ethnic minority women and older women.

Women and housing policy in Salford

Rachel's husband left her and her six children several years ago. She found it difficult to cope with the children on her own, and neighbours testify that the children were often unruly and badly behaved. But because neighbours knew the family, they were able to lend a hand, keeping them in order.

The estate that Rachel lived on was partly sold off to private developers and Rachel was offered another property in a different area which she accepted because she thought she had no alternative. However, things were never the same. The children's behaviour seemed to go from bad to worse and Rachel did not know anyone who could give her the support she wanted.

Eventually, her children were taken into care and Rachel found herself homeless. She has now obtained privately rented accommodation and has custody of two of her children. However, her new home is little better than her original home on the council estate and, without the security of a community around her, there is little hope that Rachel's housing situation will improve in the near future.

Between August 1982 and March 1990, council stock in Salford has declined by 16%, from 44,993 to 37,895. By February 1990 over 5,000 properties had been sold off to tenants under the right-to-buy legislation. A further 960 had been sold off to private developers.

In November 1989 there were 6,057 people registered on the waiting list for housing in Salford. At this time, a total of 2,688 council properties were empty. This means that, even if all empty properties were allocated, less than half of the people on the waiting list could be offered accommodation.

Because of their low incomes in comparison to men, women in Salford are constrained in their housing choices, similar to women nationally. A large number of women, therefore, turn to the council sector for housing because of a lack of other options.

Salford City Council do not currently carry out any monitoring of housing applications or allocations by sex. Consequently, they do not know the extent or the nature of demand for housing from women in Salford. The council do not, at present, have a Women's Unit or a Women's Officer attached to the Housing Department, so they have no information on the particular problems that women face regarding access to housing in Salford.

Homeless women in Salford

Bridget is a single parent with four young children. She contacted Salford Women's Aid after suffering several years of violence at the hands of her husband. Several months later Bridget was ready to leave the refuge and she contacted Salford City about being re-housed. She was offered a property quite quickly but it was in very poor condition. Bridget accepted the property anyway because she thought she would not get anything else.

However, because she had no furniture, she was unable to move in straight away and applied to the DSS for a grant from the social fund. While she was waiting her house was broken into and vandalised. Now Bridget has to wait for the repairs to be carried out and also wait to hear whether she will qualify for help with furniture.

Salford City Council does not, at present, have a detailed written policy on homelessness. The only guidelines for officers are the legal requirements. Because there is no detailed written policy, dealings with women (and men) who apply for accommodation as homeless are often on a discretionary and ad hoc basis.

Persons applying as homeless are given one offer only, while other applicants from the waiting and transfer lists are given three offers – clearly a discriminatory practice which means that homeless people have to accept whatever accommodation they are offered.

There is virtually no emergency or temporary accommodation for homeless women in Salford. There is a hostel for homeless families where women with children who are considered to be in priority need under the terms of Part III of the Housing Act can go. Salford City say the hostel may also accept single women depending on their circumstances.

A small development to house young homeless people aged 16–25 in Salford has just been completed. Five bedrooms will be available to young single women. However, there is still a desperate need for single sex accommodation for homeless women in Salford.

There are two refuges for women escaping violent partners in Salford housing just 23 women in total. Salford Women's Aid say that there is a desperate need for more refuge space for women in Salford and also more suitable move-on accommodation for women leaving the refuges. There is also a need to make the funding of existing refuges more secure: at present, the refuges are going from year to year without knowing whether they will receive funding for the following year.

They say, 'women living in the refuges are classed as "homeless" by the local authority and as such are given one offer of rehousing which they usually have to take.

These offers are the hard-to-let properties which no one else wants. Even these are taking longer and longer to acquire as the council sells off more of its properties to private developers. The offers are usually in a very bad state of repair and in need of decoration throughout...

... so, women, having made the decision to leave violent situations, are faced with a long stay in the refuge with often a poor and unsatisfactory property being offered at the end of it' (Salford Women's Aid, Annual Report 1988/89).

Refuge workers believe that the council have an unsympathetic attitude towards homeless women in Salford, and particularly, those escaping from domestic violence. One woman at a refuge applied to the council for permanent accommodation and was offered a property just four doors away from her husband. She turned the property down and was eventually rehoused by a local housing association.

Refuge workers say that, on average, between eight and nine women are turned away each week because there is no room for them. Women are normally referred to Manchester Women's Aid who act as co-ordinators for the Greater Manchester area. There are three refuges in Manchester itself with an average bed space for seven families each. Refuge workers at Manchester Women's Aid say that often all three refuges are full. In such circumstances, up to 30 women may be turned away each week. Inevitably, many women in Salford (and Manchester) return to their husbands because of a lack of alternatives.

Salford City Council say 'women with or without dependent children escaping domestic violence or threats of violence will be found suitable temporary accommodation pending further investigation of their circumstances' (letter

Moving in..views from a flat offered by the council to a woman escaping domestic violence.

...Smashed in

...Blocked in

from Salford City Council, dated 23.4.90). However Salford's housing officers must be satisfied as to the existence of actual violence or the threat of violence before other accommodation is offered. Although this is in accordance with existing legislation, it means that women may be denied secure housing at a crisis point in their lives while the council are trying to get corroborative evidence.

Black and ethnic minority women in Salford

Paramjit came recently to Britain with her husband and two young children. Her husband earns a low wage and the family had difficulty managing on their income. However, they did not speak English and did not know where to go for help. A neighbour became concerned about the welfare of the youngest child and contacted social services. A social worker visited the family and was able to provide help and advice about welfare services and benefits in Salford. However, Paramjit was one of the lucky ones. Many more black and ethnic minority families do not receive any help and do not know where to go.

Salford is traditionally a white, working class area. Here, as in Britain generally, black and ethnic minority women can face racism and discrimination in their daily contact with the white population.

There is no up-to-date information on the numbers of black and ethnic minority people in Salford. The most recent information comes from the 1981 Census which showed that 7404 people in Salford (3.19% of the population) lived in households headed by people born outside the UK and the Irish Republic.

The black and ethnic minority community in Salford includes a large Yemeni community and also the Bangladeshi, Pakistani, Chinese and Vietnamese communities.

Many black and ethnic minority people came to Salford in the 1940s and 1950s in response to the demand for labour in the docks and heavy industry. The collapse of the manufacturing base in Salford brought problems of high unemployment.

Black and ethnic minority people in Salford can face isolation, poor employment prospects, poor health and poor housing, similar to the problems faced in Britain generally. One of the main problems in Salford is that information about advice, services and resources is rarely translated into ethnic minority languages, so many people are unaware of voluntary and statutory services available in Salford.

Discussions with local advice agencies in Salford revealed that racism, harassment and abuse are common experiences for black and ethnic minority men and women in Salford today.

> **Mrs C. was harassed when her older daughter chose a black boyfriend and neighbours on the exclusively white council estate did not approve.** The family were subjected to racist taunts and one of Mrs C.'s sons was beaten up by a gang of white youths wielding baseball bats.
>
> The family applied immediately to the council for rehousing and moved into a relative's one-bedroom flat. After some weeks the council offered them a house. When the family visited the property they found it covered with racist graffiti, inside and out, and in a poor state of repair. Mrs C. rejected the offer and was eventually rehoused by a local housing association.

Racist graffiti on a housing estate in Salford.

Margaret describes herself as of mixed race. She lives alone with her young son and has been repeatedly subjected to harassment and abuse by neighbours, including damage to property, theft, racist graffiti and a physical assault on her young son. The incidents were reported to the police on three occasions but no action was taken.

Salford City do not, at present, carry out monitoring by ethnic origin, so they lack data on the demand for housing among ethnic minority communities in Salford. Salford City do not have an anti-racist policy or any procedures for dealing with racist and sexist abuse for council officers. The Housing Department does not translate any material on service provision and there are no specific grounds for eviction for racial or sexual harassment.

Salford Local Council for Voluntary Services (SLCVS) is currently working on a project, funded by the Department of Environment, exploring the needs and experiences of black people in Salford. The project arose out of preliminary research by local community workers in the area which revealed a lack of knowledge and concern among both public and voluntary agencies in the area about the black and ethnic minority communities.

The purpose of the SLCVS project is to feed back information on black and ethnic minority community needs and experiences to public and voluntary organisations, thereby improving the present situation. It is hoped that both statutory and voluntary agencies will begin to take seriously the needs and experiences of black and ethnic minority communities in Salford.

Older women in Salford

Mary is in her late 70s and lives alone in sheltered accommodation run by the council. Last year Mary had a bad fall and spent some time in hospital. She was discharged with a walking frame which she needed for several months. Mary's flat is a small, one-bedroom flat and she had difficulty moving around with her frame. In particular, the doors were not wide enough and she had to walk sideways through them. In order to get into her kitchen, Mary had to have the door completely removed.

Ethel is in her 80s and lives with her husband on the fifth floor of a high rise block of council flats. Ethel is nearly blind and also has difficulty walking. The lift in Ethel's block often breaks down which leaves her house-bound and totally dependent on her husband. Ethel wishes she lived in a low-rise flat where she could be more independent.

Social workers at a local day centre in Salford spoke about the lack of concern among policy makers and housing providers in Salford about the needs of older people in the area. Consequently, many older women are living in totally unsuitable housing.

Social workers spoke about the lack of co-ordination between public agencies in Salford who are responsible for older people. They suggested that the Housing Department were not aware of the needs of older people as they move from their own homes to sheltered accommodation and residential care.

Beatrice has to climb into her kitchen sink to change her curtains

Consequently, older people can be overlooked until crises arise.

Furthermore, there is no existing agency or body which makes regular assessments of older people in the area as their housing needs change. Staff at the day centre felt that someone within the Housing Department should take responsibility for this.

Also, staff were concerned about the suitability of housing in the area for older people. They felt that housing is not tailored to individual needs. For example, sheltered housing in the area is often built with plug sockets at the bottom of walls or light switches high up on the walls – beyond the reach of older people, especially those with restricted mobility.

Staff were concerned that, in the current situation of financial cutbacks, the quality of housing for older people is likely to suffer even more. At present, the local authority is being encouraged, along with other local authorities, to use private services if these are cheaper than publicly provided services. There was great concern that these cutbacks may be made without due concern for the quality of services and will inevitably mean even poorer quality services for older people in Salford.

Women's voices

Elaine is a single lesbian, living in a council flat and paying £30 a week in rent. Elaine is far from happy in her home. She says, '*the place is cold and damp and ... unfit for an animal ... I've lived in some places and compared to my present situation [they] can be classed as a palace ... I find also wherever I've gone I've been constantly harassed by neighbours for no reason at all and despite writing complaints to whom ever it concerns – well, not a darn thing is done.*

I find that if it's known a person is gay like myself, then people will go out to harass or even persecute the person. I know I have been through hell on a few occasions, but being the strong willed person I am, I've managed to come through everything, though at times, how hard it's been...'

Estelle is a single woman buying her own flat in Salford. She says, '*I was not happy at first living here because of its situation – I felt it would not be safe to go out at night. The street lighting is very poor and there was originally a lot of wasteland and derelict buildings round about. Most of the people [round here] have cars but if you don't, or can't, have one, then this is more of a problem..*

... The main housing problem single women have is that because mortgages are so high and women's wages are so low on average, it is almost impossible to afford to buy a flat or house just now, and [as a single woman] you are also bottom priority for council housing. I can afford [to buy] because I let the second bedroom. I get on alright with my flatmate, but I would prefer not to do this because it defeats the whole object of getting your own flat ...'

Linda lives in a ground floor flat in Greater Manchester which she is buying with a mortgage. She says, '*I sometimes feel vulnerable when I hear drunken men outside [my flat] at night. Women's needs in housing [include] better street lighting, telephones in the bedroom, locks on all doors, spyholes on the front door, window locks, preferably an alarm system but they are too expensive – ideally there should be grants available and a special security adviser from the council...the local police could make themselves known...*

...I have experienced threatening situations within the block of flats by groups of young male residents living together – noise, abuse, cans of alcohol strewn on the grass...'

Anne-Marie is a single woman living in Salford. She says, *'I feel that most single or unmarried women are never given the same status as others in terms of transfers, waiting list, etc., etc. Women on their own with, or without, children require special needs, support and understanding. In general, women are the main 'housekeepers', but are never involved at any planning level, i.e. children's play area, security lay-out of estates, design of houses, etc...*

... Although I am lucky, compared to most, I would be a lot happier if there was more daylight allowed into my house, more windows, a better and more economical heating system, better designed rooms with more space, more cupboard space, a large kitchen where we could eat – things would be a lot brighter. Why aren't there more women in planning departments and housing committees?'

The women above raise issues which need to be taken on board by decision makers, including housing design, security, discrimination and poor conditions. It is essential that housing providers and policy makers begin to listen to what women are saying about their housing needs and experiences.

Current developments in Salford City Council's policy

Salford City have recently appointed an Equal Opportunities Officer to examine service delivery in relation to equal opportunities. Among things under review is the introduction of ethnic monitoring. The review covers the homeless services in Salford and Salford City say that the particular needs of women are being given consideration.

Shelter welcomes these moves and hopes that Salford City will consider the policy recommendations below in their review of service provision.

Overall conclusions from the study

The case study has shown that the housing needs of women in Salford have not been taken seriously, as in Britain generally. Many women live in unsuitable properties and stay in situations where they are unhappy because of a lack of housing options. The needs of particular groups of women, such as black and ethnic minority women, disabled women, homeless women and older women are, at present, largely ignored.

The case study has shown that privatisation is not in the interests of women in Salford. Because of their lower incomes, women cannot generally afford to become home-owners without a male partner in Salford, as in Britain generally.

As the council sector in Salford is depleted, through right-to-buy sales and wholesale privatisation, less accommodation will be available to women in need.

Salford City's planned review of housing services and provision, in which the particular needs of women are being given consideration, is to be welcomed. It is time that housing providers and policy makers in Salford, and within Britain generally, began to take the housing needs and experiences of women seriously ■

POLICY RECOMMENDATIONS FOR SALFORD CITY COUNCIL

1. Salford City must halt and reverse trends in privatising council housing in Salford. Our research has shown that privatisation is not meeting the needs of women in Salford.

2. Salford City must urgently produce a comprehensive written homelessness policy and detailed guidelines for council officers. The policy should include an equal opportunities statement.

3. All council officers should be trained in equal opportunities awareness and practice.

4. Salford City should urgently introduce procedures to monitor allocations, transfers, waiting lists and homeless applications by age, disability, ethnic origin, sex and sexuality wherever possible.

5. Salford City should set up a Women's Unit or Women's Officer to assess demand for housing from women in Salford and ensure that their needs are being met. The Women's Unit or Officer could also act as an advice service to women in the area.

   The Women's Unit or Women's Officer should liaise with local women's organisations and community and voluntary organisations, and social workers working with targeted groups. These groups should include black and ethnic minority women, disabled women, lesbians and older women.

6. Salford City should urgently consider rehousing people in targeted groups who are found to be living in unsuitable conditions. Regular assessments

of needs should be made, in conjunction with other bodies, to ensure the council is continuing to meet local needs.

7. Salford City should make funding available for adaptations to properties occupied by disabled people.

8. Salford City should ensure all material on service provision is translated into ethnic minority languages.

9. Salford City should include in tenancy agreements a statement that sexual and racial harassment and harassment on the grounds of sexuality constitutes a breach of the agreement. There should be a clear policy of sanctions, including eviction, in the event of a breach on these grounds.

10. Salford City should draw up a formal policy for rehousing people who have been racially or sexually harassed, where those people wish to be rehoused.

11. Salford City should urgently make funds available to ensure the provision of single-sex emergency accommodation for homeless women in Salford.

12. Salford City should consider providing funds for an additional refuge for women escaping violence and also some form of 'move on' or 'second stage' accommodation for women escaping violence.

13. Salford City should increase and make more secure the funding of existing refuges ■

CONCLUSION

This report has pointed out that women are disadvantaged in access to housing in comparison to men, and that current housing policies mean women are losing out even more. Independent access to housing has always been difficult for women, and yet over the last decade, women's housing options have been reduced even further.

Part I of the report suggested that the housing needs of women in Britain are not being taken seriously by housing providers and policy makers. The needs of particular groups of women, such as black and ethnic minority women, disabled women, lesbians, older women, single women, women escaping violence and young women are, at present, largely ignored. The Salford case study showed that the housing needs of women in Salford have not yet been taken seriously, as in Britain generally.

The report has shown that privatisation is not in women's interests. Women cannot generally afford to become home-owners in their own right and women, more than men, rely on council housing because of a lack of other housing options. So women lose out most by the reduction of council housing provision. The Salford case study, which focused on the effects of privatisation on women's access to housing, has confirmed that women are losing out because of privatisation policies.

Women are disadvantaged in the housing market both because of their low incomes and also because their particular problems are not addressed by decision makers. It is time that both policy makers and housing providers began to redress the balance ■

APPENDIX

Research methodology

The questionnaire survey was conducted during January and February 1990 and involved calling at all the properties on the Trinity estate (including the St. Stephen St. area) of which 375 were found to be occupied. Two-hundred and twenty-four households agreed to be interviewed – a response rate of 60%.

Of the respondents, 63% (141) were council tenants, 28% (63) were owner-occupiers, five per cent (11) were renting from a housing association and four per cent (eight) were renting from private landlords. These figures correspond closely to the tenure breakdown on the estate.

A record was kept of the location and type of all the properties on the estate. This was checked at the end of the survey and it was found that the respondents were evenly spread across the estate. It is, therefore, believed that the sample and the views expressed are representative of the households living on the estate.

Additional qualitative data was gathered about women's housing needs in Salford through interviews with women's organizations, advice agencies and individual women in Salford. Some of the information was used for individual case studies. In order to protect the women referred to, names and any identifiable features have been changed ∎

BIBLIOGRAPHY

Almack, C. and Prendergast, Y., *Belittled and Bewildered*, Shelter and Nottinghamshire Homeless Action, 1989.

Anlin, S., *Out but not Down! – The Housing Needs of Lesbians*, Homeless Action, 1989.

Argyle, K., "Privatisation in Salford", *Christian Action Journal*, Winter 1988.

Austerberry, H. and Watson, S., "A Woman's Place: A Feminist Approach to Housing in Britain", *Feminist Review*, Summer 1982.

Basterfield, D., *Women and Housing*, Ealing Council, September 1988.

Becker, S., *Social Fund Project Report*, Benefits Research, July 1989.

Binney, V. et al, *Leaving Violent Men*, Manchester Women's Aid Federation, 1981.

Bonnerjea, L. and Lawton, J., *No Racial Harassment This Week: A Study Undertaken in the London Borough of Brent*, Policy Studies Institute, 1988.

Booth, A., *Raising the Roof on Housing Myths*, Shelter, 1989.

Bowes, A., *Ethnic Minority Housing Problems in Glasgow*, University of Stirling, 1989.

Bradford, M.G. and Steward, A., *Inner City Refurbishment: An evaluation of private-public partnership schemes*, CUPS No.3., Manchester University, September 1988.

Bradshaw, J., *Lone Parents: Policy in the Doldrums*, Occasional Paper No.9., Family Policy Studies Centre, 1989.

Brailey, M., *Women's Access to Council Housing*, Occasional Paper No. 25, The Planning Exchange, Glasgow, 1987.

Brion, M. and Tinker, A., *Women in Housing: Access and Influence*, Housing Centre Trust, 1980.

Bristol City Council and WISH, *Single Women and Homelessness in Bristol*, 1988.

Brown, C., *Black and White Britain: The Third PSI Survey*, Heineman, 1984.

Burrows, L., *The Housing Act 1988: A Shelter Guide*, Shelter, 1989.

Burrows, L. and Hunter N., *Forced Out: Harassment and Illegal Eviction*, Shelter, 1990.

Care and Repair, *Annual Report*, 1989.

CHAR, *Housing for Lesbians and Gays* (background papers), CHAR, 1988.

CHAR, *Housing for Lesbians and Gay Men* (conference report), CHAR, 1988.

City of Salford, *Trinity Project Area Profile (Ref. TR1 AAA) Report*, undated.

City of Salford, Housing Department, written correspondence from City Housing Manager, dated 23.4.90.

City of Salford, *Social Survey*, 1985.

City of Salford, *Report to the Housing Committee*, November 22nd, 1985.

Clarke, E., *Young Single Mothers Today*, National Council for One-Parent Families, 1989.

Clarke, K., *Black and Ethnic Minority Women in Britain: A Statistical Overview*, EOC, unpublished paper, 1988.

Commission for Racial Equality, *Race and Mortgage Lending – Report of a Formal Investigation* (Rochdale), CRE, 1985.

Commission for Racial Equality, *Living in Terror*, CRE, 1987.

Commission for Racial Equality, *Homelessness and Discrimination*, CRE, 1988.

Cosgrave, A., *Young and Homeless in London*, Housing Services Agency, 1988.

Dale, J. and Foster, P., *Feminists and State Welfare*, RKP, 1986.

Department of Environment, *Local Authorities' Action under the Homelessness Provisions of the 1985 Housing Act: Results for the fourth quarter 1989*, March 1990.

Ealing Council, *The Race Implications of the Housing Bill: Report of a Conference*, Ealing Council and Federation of Black Housing Organisations, April 1989.

Eardley, T., *Move-On Housing*, National Federation of Housing Associations, 1989.

Employment Gazette, Department of Employment, 1988.

English House Condition Survey 1986, Department of Environment, HMSO 1988.

Equal Opportunities Commission, *Women and Men in Britain*, EOC, 1989.

Family Policy Studies Centre, *Community Care 2000*, FPSC, 1989.

Finer R. M., *Report to the Committee on One Parent Families*, HMSO, 1974.

First Stop, Shelter and Leeds Citizens Advice Bureau, *The Increasing Links between Poverty and Homelessness amongst Under-18s due to Recent Changes in Social Security Legislation*, Shelter Report, 1989.

Friedman, D. and Pawson, H., *One in Every Hundred*, London Housing Unit, 1989.

General Household Survey 1986, HMSO, 1989.

General Household Survey 1987, HMSO, 1989.

Gilbert, J., *Not Just A Roof: Single Homeless Women's Housing Needs in Birmingham*, Birmingham Standing Conference For The Single Homeless, 1986.

Glasgow Council for Single Homeless, *Single Homeless in Glasgow*, 1988.

Gosling, J., *Young Homelessness: A National Scandal*, Young Homelessness Group, 1989.

Graham, H., *Caring for the Family*, Health Education Council, 1986.

Greater London Council, *Private Tenants in London: 1983/4 Survey*, GLC, 1986.

Hendessi, M., *Migrants: The Invisible Homeless*, London Voluntary Service Council, 1987.

Home Office, *Racial Attacks*, HMSO, 1981.

Housing Construction Statistics, September 1989, HMSO 1989.

Housing Advice Switchboard, *Annual Report*, 1989.

Joint Docklands Action Group, *Housing in the Docklands*, JDAG, 1987.

Labour Force Survey, Department of Employment, 1987.

Lickiss, R., *Housing and Women in Brighton and Hove: A Local Examination of National Housing Issues*, Urban Studies Centre, Brighton Polytechnic, 1987.

Local Government Information Unit, *Caring for People: The Government's Plans for Care in the Community*, Special Briefing No.32, LGIU, 1990.

Logan, F., *Homelessness and Relationship Breakdown*, National Council for One-Parent Families, 1986.

London Research Centre, *The London Housing Survey 1986-7*, London Research Centre, 1989.

London Housing News, London Housing Unit, April 1988.

Low Pay Unit, *The Poor Decade: Wage Inequality in the 1980s*, LPU, 1988.

Mama, A., "Violence against Black Women," *Feminist Review 32*, 1989.

May, J., *Estate Regeneration Or Community Destruction?*, Cambridge University, 1989.

Morris, J., *Freedom to Lose: Housing Policy and People with Disabilities*, Shelter briefing, 1988.

Morris, J., *The Impact on Women of National Housing Policy since 1979 and Prospects for the Future*, Shelter, 1987.

Morris, J. "Keeping Women in their Place", *Roof*, July/August 1988.

Morris, J., *Our Homes, Our Rights: Housing, Independent Living and Physically Disabled People*, Shelter, 1990.

Morris, J. and Winn, M., *Housing and Social Inequality*, Hilary Shipman, 1990 (forthcoming).

National Association of Young People In Care, *Abuse in the Care System*, 1990.

National Cyrenians, *Women and Homelessness: An Analysis*, 1984.

Nationwide Anglia Building Society, *Lending to Women: Annual Report*, 1989.

Newman, C., *Young Runaways*, The Children's Society, 1989.

Niner, P. & Thomas, A., *Living in Temporary Accommodation*, Department of Employment, 1989.

Oldman, J., *Facts and Figures on Homelessness*, Joint Charities Group on Homelessness, 1989.

OPCS Disability Survey, *Report One: The Prevalence of Disability among Adults*, HMSO, 1988.

OPCS Disability Survey, *Report Two: The Financial Circumstances of Disabled Adults Living in Private Households*, HMSO, 1988.

Pahl, J., *The Allocation of Money and the Structuring of Inequality within Marriage*, Health Services Research Unit, University of Kent, 1982.

Pahl, J., *Money and Marriage*, Macmillan, 1990.

Pascall, G., *Social Policy: A Feminist Analysis*, Tavistock, 1986.

Randall, G., *Homeless and Hungry: A Sign of the Times*, Centrepoint Soho, 1989.

Rao, N., *Black Women in Public Sector Housing*, Black Women and Housing Group, CRE, 1990.

Russel, M., *Taking Stock: Refuge Provision in London in the late 1980s*, Southwark Council, 1985.

Salford Women's Aid, *Annual Report*, 1989.

Salvation Army, *Interim Report, The Faces of Homelessness in London*, Department of Psychology, University of Surrey, 1989.

Scottish Council for Single Homeless, *Women's Homelessness: The Hidden Problem*, SCCH, 1989.

Shelter/MORI, *Housing for Young People* , 1987.

Shrimpton, C., *Appraisal of Local Authority Responses to Domestic Violence*, unpublished research paper, 1988.

Simpson, A., *Stacking the Decks*, Nottingham and District Community Relations Council, 1981.

Smith, L., *Domestic Violence: An Overview of the Literature*, HMSO, 1987.

Social Trends, HMSO, 1990.

Steele, A., *A Research Report on Homeless Women in Newcastle*, University of Newcastle, 1989.

Stevens L. et al, *Ethnic Minorities and Building Society Lending in Leeds*, Leeds Community Relations Council, 1981.

Strathdee, R., *Nobody Wants To Know*, Gingerbread, 1989.

Venn, S., *Singled Out: Local Authority Policies for Single People*, CHAR, 1985.

Watson, S. and Austerberry, H., *Housing and Homelessness: A Feminist Perspective*, RKP, 1986.

Women's National Commission, *Lone Parent Families*, Cabinet Office, 1989.